THE
LANGUAGE
OF
TRUST

DIALOGUE OF THE GENERATIONS

THE LANGUAGE OF TRUST

DIALOGUE OF THE GENERATIONS

Douglas Holmes, Ph.D.
Monica Bychowski Holmes, Ph.D.
Lisa Appignanesi, Ph.D.

SCIENCE HOUSE, INC.

Designed by Jennifer Mellen

Library of Congress Catalog Card Number: 76–172939
Standard Book Number: 87668–049–X

Manufactured in the United States of America

To the memory of *Margaret* and *Myron*
To *Maria* and *Gustav*
To *Hannah* and *Aron*

〜〜〜〜〜〜〜〜〜〜〜〜〜〜〜〜〜〜〜〜〜〜〜〜

PARENTS ALL

CONTENTS

FOREWORD

The authorship of any book can be regarded as an adventure in communication. After all, the writer's task is to transcend his own personalized experience so that his thoughts can become part of the public, shared consciousness. While the first step in the process of communication is that of providing information, this is not sufficient in and of itself. In a book such as this it is crucial that the reader perceive himself as a participant, actual or potential, in the subject matter presented.

Among many social scientists conducting community studies and programs today there is a growing frustration born of our inability to communicate meaningfully with those whom we wish to reach. Many of us suffer from what might be termed professional inarticulation: we speak easily and often to our professional colleagues through journals and papers regarding our findings and our future research plans. Yet when it comes to communicating these results and their implications to the most important group in terms of social change — the general public — we are suddenly mute. While there is need for communication among social scientists, there is an even greater need to contact non-professional groups. This need becomes a responsibility when research and programs are funded publicly.

Currently there is a growing interest among social scientists in "research utilization." In an effort to make our particular research and clinical experience useful, we at the Center for Community Research have initiated a collaboration with Dr. Lisa Appignanesi, a professional writer. Thus, this book is the product of a union between the social sciences and literature. This particular collaboration constitutes something of an experiment, an "adventure," to learn whether such a combination of disciplines can become an established method of approach in seeking to facilitate communication. Through the full-time engagement of a professional writer, the Center for Community Research hopes to establish a model that will be adopted in other such settings.

This book is an outgrowth of our experience in consultation and treatment with many adolescents and their families; it is also the outgrowth of an NIMH-supported study of drug use among hippies and matched groups of non-hippies.[1] Therefore, it is based on the work of a number of people on the staff of the Center for Community Research. We would like most especially to acknowledge the contributions of our social workers Janet Geller and Lester Marks, our graduate students in psychology Arlene Friedman and Susan Jaffe, and our consulting psychiatrist Richard Rabkin. For three years they have contributed not only their work but their ideas and considerable talents to the Center's involvement with families as well. Similarly, we would like to acknowledge the work of the Center's Director of Field Services, Theo Solomon, who played a principal part in the implementation of the study on hippies.

Finally, no Research Center can function without its research assistants and secretaries. We would most particularly like to thank Laura Fisher and Bonnie Clips who assisted in the data collection, and Mary Emsworth, Kathy Kinzel, and Catherine Presky, without whose endless good humor, good will, and secretarial contribution this book would not have been possible.

The Authors

[1] The research and programs upon which certain portions of this book are based were supported, in part, by the National Institute of Mental Health (Grant # ROIMH 16161-01) and by the New York City Community Mental Health Board (contract #400019 . We wish also to thank for their cooperation those community centers of the Associated YM-YWHA's of Greater New York which participated in our research and programs.

PREFACE

Much has been said and written about the conflict between parent and child, adult and adolescent, particularly in recent years. Our media men have rediscovered the generational struggle as a newsworthy item, and they have packaged the concept and written pages of advertising around it, thus magnifying its importance. They have presented it to us with a bright, attractive, and readily remembered label: "generation gap" — the magic formula, the abracadabra of our era, to be applied in all instances of generational stress. When a father is confronted by his son's seemingly inexplicable determination to drop out of high school, he conjures up the wisdom of the term "generation gap" and his conscience is put easily to rest. When a mother cannot immediately comprehend the significance of a Bob Dylan lyric, her daughter shrugs her shoulders, retreats, and exclaims, "It's because of the generation gap!" When a university student body supported by its faculty protests the administration's intransigence on any number of issues, the administrators once again have recourse to the "generation gap" as a pat explanation of their inability to establish a dialogue.

But the label attached to a problem doesn't constitute its solution. The prevalence of the term "generation gap" has only succeeded in grossly concretizing a subtle demarcation line over which the two groups rail in hostility. From the standpoint of adults, the "generation gap" has banded together the young in an amorphous group, severed them from adult society, and distanced them in a dehumanized, alien throng. A voice from the young is a voice from the "other side," the enemy in his media-defined uniform of long hair and jeans, puffing away at a "joint."

From the camp of the young, it is the adult world and the "establishment" which constitutes the enemy. This "other side" of the "generation gap" appears as an equally anonymous mass, armed and threatening. With machine-like precision, this adult band crushes any form of dissent and renders ineffective all actions not programmed in its methodical thrust.

The traditional struggle between the generations has been emphasized and mystified to such a degree that we have lost all sense of the human reality beneath the television myth and the newspaper abstraction. Who are the individual youths behind the faceless, stoned media "hippies" or the Chicago rebels? Who are the individual adults and parents of Spiro Agnew's silent majority or the bland-eyed urban liberals? The mass stereotypes created for us and maintained by our unquestioning attitude have obscured the living beings. Before any viable bridge can be constructed across the "generation gap," it is essential that we recognize both adults and youths as individual persons who share daily tasks and problems. This is not to minimize the differences between the generations, which in our rapidly changing world are necessarily great, but rather to enhance awareness of shared humanity, so that mass hostility can be diminished and individual problems realistically confronted.

The purpose of this book, then, is to present adults to youths and youths to adults in an attempt to create a language of mutual trust and understanding within the family. It is within the family that the generational conflict has its roots, and it is here that the seeds of a dialogue must be planted. We have no illusions that the conflict can be eliminated. This would be as undesirable as it is impossible, for the conflict between youth and age is basic to individual maturation. However, the family should provide a shelter for its members, launching them into the turmoil of the external world while remaining in itself a place of warmth and essential security. When the father of a drug-taking youngster feels he is harboring an alien, a criminal, under his roof; when the youth feels his parents to be incomprehending judges; and the formula "generation gap" gives sanction to their enmity, mistrust and guarded hostility usurp the role of the family.

In this book, aimed at both parents and their youngsters, we are setting out to define, and to describe in practical terms, some of the major problems which the family containing adolescents, say from the ages of twelve to eighteen, confronts. We hope that by re-introducing one to the other in personal terms, by describing the world which each inhabits, and providing some model dialogues — clues toward establishing closer communication — a step in the direction of familial harmony will be taken.

This book does not attempt to deal with the problems of economically impoverished families. That is, the problems of the culture of poverty are so different that they would require a separate book to do them justice. Hence, this book is about, and for, middle-class adolescents and their parents.

One major distinguishing point between adolescents and parents today lies in their relationship to drugs and all that the drug culture has come to imply. It is widely acknowledged that a great many adolescents today take drugs. In some areas of the country, the drug experience will begin at an early age; in the majority of areas, the youth will have come into contact with drugs by the time he leaves high school. This is a fact which parents must recognize and accustom themselves to before any dialogue can be set up with the young. Your adolescent child probably will have tried either marijuana, the psychedelics, "ups" and "downs," the amphetamines, or the barbiturates. His relationship to drugs may be a casual one. It may not be. In either case, the parent as well as the adolescent must familiarize himself with the makeup and the effects of various drugs, and determine at which point drug use shades into abuse for each individual youngster.

Our viewpoint, based on extensive work with the contemporary adolescent, is that drug taking, because of the nature of the cultural experience of today's youngster, is *incidental* to his personality development. Drugs do not create a new kind of personality — they merely create new problems which both parents and teenagers must confront realistically. We are not concerned with making a plea for the legalization of marijuana, nor do we condone "scare" tactics to warn parents and teenagers of the encroaching dangers of drug taking. We do insist, however, that a realistic appraisal of the drug situation is necessary for parents if they are to establish a dialogue with their children, and similarly that adolescents try to understand the validity of their parents' fears about drugs.

In our attempt to personalize the factions on either side of the "generation gap," we have constructed in the first two chapters several model case histories, first of adolescents, then of parents. These case histories are composite ones, based loosely on actual case records and enlarged by our observations of parents and teen-agers in consultation service settings. Since it is unfeasible to explore all the possibilities of individual experience, we have had to resort to models or types of behavior; but we have tried to incorporate into these models illustrations of the most common questions and problems youngsters and their parents come to us with, together with the most frequently repeated reactions to tense family situations. If parents and youngsters can recognize themselves in these profiles and see the ramifications of their actions, the models will have served their purpose.

We also explore the larger social issues that distinguish the generations. If parents are to understand their children, they must understand the forces and the philosophies underlying the life style of the so-called counter culture. Conversely, adolescents must try to comprehend what makes their parents act the way they do, so that adults may take on a three-dimensional fullness in their eyes, rather than remaining flat shadow puppets manipulated by a blindly irrational and authoritarian system.

An anatomy of the drug world follows. Though several recent books have done much to clarify misconceptions about the various kinds of drugs — the extent and nature of their usage together with their effects — we feel that it is necessary in a book aimed at the family to examine the facts and fallacies of the drug mystique. Much of our data is based on information gathered by the Center for Community Research in a research study of drug use. Should the trend toward increased drug use continue — and there is no reason to believe it won't — then it is imperative that parents know as much about drugs as their children and that adolescents be thoroughly informed about the nature of the herbs and chemicals that they are taking into their systems.

We present a series of model dialogues between parents and adolescents in the last part of this book. These dialogues provide examples of how the two groups can enter into closer communication, if contact and understanding are lacking. There are, of course, no set ways in which parents can approach their children, or vice versa, but one can learn certain techniques to minimize hostility.

Many will say that things are indeed rotten in the state of America when outsiders must step in to mediate between parents and children. It is only too natural for parents to resent this kind of intrusion and thrust this book aside. But our experience has shown us that in many families today alienation between parent and teenager has reached such a degree of intensity that all possibilities of promoting a relationship must be entertained. We have as yet in our society found no structure to replace the family unit, despite its present state of embattlement. Thus we must attempt to make the family a place of not only material, but emotional, security and communal trust, from which the child can garner sufficient strength to meet the complexities and tensions of our world. If this book can help to build even the slightest bridge between the generations and help to create a language of trust in the family, then it will have served its purpose.

Sounds lik fluff.

THE LANGUAGE OF TRUST

DIALOGUE OF THE GENERATIONS

PROFILES
OF THE
CONTEMPORARY
ADOLESCENT

ANNA

Fifteen-year-old Anna pulled on her snugly fitting jeans and gazed at herself in the mirror. She had no desire to go to school this morning, sit through a few more boring periods, and attempt to escape questioning on work she had barely prepared. Really, balancing chemistry equations seemed a stupid task when she had so many more important things to worry about. Once again the idea of dropping out next year and getting a job flitted hazily through her mind; but no, she mustn't think about that. She did really want to go to college. It was a question of holding out for a few more years. She thought of Gregory, and wondered if he had gone home last night after leaving her or if he had returned to the party. Gregory was definitely becoming a problem. She had been seeing him fairly regularly for two months now, and she knew that if she didn't go to bed with him soon and consolidate their relationship, he would go the way of all her other boy friends. She couldn't understand why she was holding out. After all, most of her friends had already shed their laughable virginity. And she did like Gregory, but . . .

Anna heard her mother calling her from the kitchen. She gave her hair a final brush stroke, examined herself one last time in the mirror, and dashed off. Her mother, pouring a cup of coffee, greeted her with a series of exclamations.

"Anna, take a look at yourself. Must you wear those old jeans every day? After we bought you all those expensive clothes. And the rings under your eyes! What time did you come in last night? Sid, Sid just look at your daughter . . . (Sid grunted from behind his morning paper.) Have you been running around with that gang of dirty hippies again? Really, Anna, you *are* going to be the death of me!"

[handwritten margin note: This is exaggerated + seems very transparent on the writers part.]

Anna wondered when, if ever, her mother would change her morning litany. She imagined that she must look rather unappealing in comparison to the smartly tailored woman beside her. But how Anna could in any way hasten the death of this energetic being who did not look a day over thirty was beyond her. And how this sophisticated woman who worked in a Manhattan lawyer's office could have such ridiculous notions about hippies was a complete mystery. Anna started to protest that her friends were not hippies and even if they were . . . but she thought better of it. Why waste her breath? Her parents wouldn't understand and her mother already seemed to be thinking of something else. Anna put aside her barely nibbled toast and stalked out of the kitchen. Her mother called out to her, "Wait, Anna, we'll give you a lift," but Anna was already half way out of the house.

The sun was breaking through the clouds and the world had begun to look a little less gray, so Anna decided to walk to school. The walk would clear her mind, and she felt like being alone, rather than crowded into the sweaty atmosphere of a rush-hour bus. At the corner, she passed a group of young construction workers. She could sense their eyes boring through her, undressing her. She imagined how they were comparing her to other women who had passed the spot. Feeling embarrased, she stumbled awkwardly, then quickened her pace. Sometimes she wished she were still a child and could stroll down the streets unnoticed.

Could the men intuit that she was still a virgin? No, that would be too much. If these things were so irrevocably transparent, then her father would know as soon as she had slept with a man, and that was preposterous. She couldn't believe it! But maybe fathers were different. She was sure that her father had never thought of her — if he thought of her at all — as anything but a rather dowdy child whom one brought presents for after periods of absence. She glanced back at the construction workers. They were still laughing among themselves, probably at the way she had stumbled. She became painfully aware of all her limbs and walking became increasingly difficult. It occurred to her that men were odious creatures.

She remembered a television program she had watched with her parents a few nights back. On it some people whose names she had forgotten were discussing women's liberation. An attractive young woman had argued that men had always kept women down and had treated them not as fellow human beings but as sexual objects, either to be pampered like pretty poodles or abused. She hadn't been too sure what the woman had meant, but now, thinking back on the construction workers, the idea struck a chord in her.

Her father, she remembered, had laughed loudly at the program and had then bitterly exclaimed, "Yes, that's why we work for them until we have a stroke, and then leave them with the life insurance! Women!" Her mother had sat quietly, not commenting. It was quite unlike her. Anna wondered what her mother thought about the whole thing and wished she could sit down and talk to her for once. She wanted to ask her about pills and contraception and men and a hundred things. But as soon as they saw each other, there was always an argument over some trivial matter. And her mother hassled her over her clothes, coming in late, the people she thought she was hanging out with, and her marks, and made her feel guilty about things which weren't even under her control.

Anna stood in front of the school. It struck her, as it did every morning, that the school looked like nothing so much as a prison — the barred windows, the cheerless façade. Inside, the long, drab corridors stretched as far as the eye could see, relieved only by the uniform doors, shutting in those who would rather be elsewhere. It was positively inhuman to be confronted by chemistry several mornings a week. And oh, that chemistry teacher! There was another odious male with his greasy hair and fawning manners. How people like that ever imagined they had anything to teach . . . and the rages he would fly into when he caught anyone passing notes or talking in class! He must realize that it was physically impossible to sit through one of his periods without some form of distraction.

Maybe today time would pass quickly. Next period there would be English, and she rather liked the teacher. He was new and a little shy, and had them read different kinds of books. She had even written a book report for him on *Native Son* that she hoped he would like. Anna wondered what her parents would say if she started dating a black boy, but of course, she knew. They would probably lock her up at home or send her to another school. It was amazing how parents thought they could shut out the real world.

Anna stopped herself in astonishment. She realized that she had been daydreaming about someone other than Gregory. Maybe she didn't like Gregory as much as she thought. But then why had she been thinking about him constantly until today? Of course there would be many other men in her life, or at least she hoped so. But for the moment it was a kind of betrayal. Had Gregory come to school today? He had been absent so often lately. She was seriously worried about him — he really was doing too many drugs these days. They would have to talk about that when they met after school.

The period had begun. Anna listlessly copied a few equations into her notebook. These figures had nothing at all to do with her. Perhaps if she concentrated very hard they would reveal some kind of magical significance; maybe if she did chemistry on acid, equations would take on a mystical aura. Gregory and she had taken some LSD on Saturday. She had enjoyed this first acid trip, but she didn't particularly want to trip again too soon. She knew that acid could be dangerous, and coming down was depressing. She had been very tired the next day and she didn't really feel it was worth it. But Gregory — oh, Gregory . . .

Suddenly she noticed that Cindy was trying to catch her attention. Beautiful Cindy had been late again today. Anna knew that her friend was having trouble at home. It seemed to be their lot to be hassled by parents. But Cindy worried Anna. She was making it with an older crowd and seemed to be having more than her share of adventures. Cindy looked particularly up tight today. Anna let her pen fall to the floor and in reaching to pick it up retrieved the letter Cindy had dropped there for her. Three sheets of closely written paper folded in eighths. Anna began to read to the drone of the teacher's voice.

"Wow! Have I had a weekend! Mom made me come to school, though I'm not feeling up to it. Met Joel on the street Saturday afternoon and he asked me to come for a drive with him, so I did. Hadn't seen him for ages and we had a good rap. Ended up at some guy's place and there was a wierd party going on. All kinds of stuff

22

in the place, grass, pills, acid. Think there was even some H floating around. Joel and I turned on. Felt good. Then we started making it. I heard some loud noises upstairs but paid no attention. This big guy came over to us and told Joel to beat it. Said I was a good looking chick and he wanted to make it with me. He was terribly aggressive. Joel said, O.K. man, O.K. cool it — and wandered off. There I was, left with this wierd stranger who started pulling at my blouse. I felt pretty freaky, but didn't know what to do. Wanted to run but didn't. Anyhow, this guy came down on me hard and suddenly I heard voices scheaming, 'The fuzz, the fuzz,' and everyone started running in all directions. I ended up in this closet and . . ."

Anna didn't want to read anymore. Cindy really frightened her at times. She wondered if she could get herself into similar situations and guessed that she was a little too careful. Sure, she had turned on plenty of times at parties. Everyone did and you couldn't be the one square. But grass seemed to have little effect on her. Just made everyone feel nice and cozy and together. She had always turned on with fairly good friends, though.

The bell rang and Anna had no time to reply to Cindy's note. She wanted to discuss Cindy with Gregory and she prayed he hadn't taken any ups this morning. It occurred to her that in the whole time she had been seeing Gregory, he had only been straight twice. And then he had been very quiet and seemed uncomfortable. She flashed that their scheduled dates consisted mostly of turning on together. Anna didn't feel it really made that much difference, but maybe Gregory didn't like her when he was straight. She must really ask him about that.

Anna enjoyed her English class. That teacher was really very good. He made you feel like a human being who had important ideas to express. They had discussed what it means to be a teenager today and Anna saw certain thoughts beginning to clarify in her mind. The teacher had praised her book report and she felt she wanted to do many more. It was at times like this that the idea of going to college took on some reality.

The morning pressed on and eventually disappeared. Gregory was waiting for her at their usual meeting place at noon. No, he hadn't been in school that morning. What was the use? School was pointless, said Gregory belligerently, an obsolete institution, created for brainwashing young people, indoctrinating them into the system and eliminating the joy from their lives. At moments like this, Anna came under Gregory's spell. He had an endless list of complaints about his parents, school, the cops, and she half agreed with everything he said. But if things were unremittingly black, what did he care for in life? Gregory terminated his tirade. Anna asked him, half hesitatingly, whether he had gone back to the party last night. He had, and a good thing, too. He had managed to buy a large supply of grass and pills at a very fair price. Since there was no one home at his place, he asked her to come over for a quiet afternoon of music together.

Anna agreed. She told Gregory she wanted to talk some things over with him. "What's up?" he wanted to know.

Anna blushed a little at his glance, not knowing how to begin. She searched for a way into the subject.

"Gregory, what . . . what do you want out of life?"

"You, woman," he teased.

"That's not what I meant. Seriously, Gregory."

He gave her a sidelong glance. "Come on, we'll go home and turn on. You'll feel better. And we'll have a good rap, O.K.?"

Anna knew what that meant. She protested.

"Gregory, we always turn on. Let's just talk for once . . . straight!" She had an inspiration. "It'll be a new kind of high."

He looked at her skeptically. "Look, Anna, I feel better when I've smoked. Things don't seem so gray. They take on color. And my head clears. I can see inside myself. I can *feel* inside you. It's good, Anna, it's good."

Anna lied a little. "But Gregory, I don't think I've ever seen you for more than an hour when you haven't been stoned on something . . . . Aren't you interested in anything besides drugs?"

"Sure, kid, sure. I told you. You. People. That's what I'm interested in. And drugs help me to appreciate you. When I'm not on something, the world looks dead. I feel dead. Look, what's all this about, anyway? Your parents haven't been on your back, have they? And don't kid yourself, Anna, there's no natural purity in this world. Everyone's on something. Your father takes tranquilizers, doesn't he? We drink coffee. We breathe this polluted air. So stop worrying. We had a good trip together the other day, right? Come on, we'll smoke and you'll loosen up."

Anna was not totally convinced, but she went with him. At Gregory's door he let her in quietly and took her up to his room. The curtains were closed and the air was filled with the soft, slightly sweet scent of grass. Gregory took his jacket and shoes off and put on a record. Anna had been here before, but always with other people. Now the sense of intimacy in the room somewhat overcame her, and she stood a little uncomfortably to the side. She had forgotten all the important things she wanted to discuss with Gregory.

Instead, her eyes fixed themselves on a corner of the room where a pile of soiled clothes lay with one black crumpled sock at the top of the heap. She heard some twangy, plaintive tones emerging from two distinct places in the room. "See him wasted on the sidewalk / in his jacket and his jeans / Never knowing if believing is a blessing or a curse / Or if the going up is worth the coming down." *

Going up. Coming down. Going up. Coming down. The words resounded uncannily in her ears. Out of the corner of her eye she could see Gregory rolling a joint. Then he was at her side, offering it to her. Going up. Coming down. She took a long drag of the loosely packed cigarette. Gregory reached for her coat and placed it on a chair. Gently folding her hand in his, he pulled her down to the floor beside him. They sat smoking quietly. Anna imagined the smoke winding its way slowly through her body. She leaned back, resting her shoulders against the bed. Her eyes were still fixed on the heap of soiled clothes.

Gregory curled his arm around her. "Isn't that better, Anna?" His fingers played in her hair and distantly she heard him murmuring, "Soft, soft . . . " The cigarette passed between them. Then Gregory rolled another.

Suddenly Anna leaped to her feet. She could feel herself subsiding into the warmth, the comfort, of the atmosphere and wanted to fight it. She had wanted a kind of confrontation with Gregory, not another afternoon of pleasant sensations. But she didn't want to force issues which maybe she was exaggerating. She walked clumsily to the window, drew back the curtain a little and gazed out on the backyards of hundreds of similar houses.

"What's with you today, Anna?"

Gregory was annoyed. Anna turned and looked at him. She could see him very clearly, each of his features etched in the narrow beam of midafternoon light poking its way through the window. But at the same time it was as if she were at some great distance, removed from the cloistered walls of the room, and seeing Gregory as a stranger. She wondered if it was the effect of the grass or the strange mood which had been with her since this morning. She saw the

* ©The Combine Music Corp., 1970

length of Gregory's legs, stretched before him; the shoulder blades faintly visible through his loose shirt; his fleshy nose and wide brown eyes, ever so slightly too close together; the ash blond hair covering his forehead and framing his face, now puzzled.

Going up. Coming down. Anna felt a rush of words pouring through her and organizing themselves in an unaccustomed lucidity.

"Gregory, we can't just spend our days going up and coming down, going up and coming down. We . . . "

Gregory interrupted. "Anna, don't lay a lecture on me. You're beginning to sound like my mother. Sit down and relax. You're incredibly up tight today. Cool it. Take it easy. Here, I'll get you something to drink and some food." Gregory stretched to his full height and walked from the room.

Anna sat down on the bed. Maybe Gregory was right. Maybe she was just up tight today, asking too many questions because of the discussion in English class. Gregory walked in holding some chocolate bars and cokes. He really was the most attractive guy she had ever dated. She bit off a big piece of chocolate. Good, very good. Perhaps that's what was wrong with her. She dimly remembered that she had had almost nothing to eat all day.

"Better?" Gregory asked. She nodded. "Stop worrying, woman. Tomorrow isn't important. It's NOW that counts. This moment, O.K.?" She nodded again and lay back. Gregory put another record on. The exotic tones of the sitar filled the room, with the peculiar whine of the shenai answering, merging.

Anna felt that hours had passed . . . but no, she could still see a gleam of light through the curtains. Yes, it *was* Gregory at her side looking playfully at her like a small boy.

"Happy?" he asked softly.

She nodded, smiling. But she could hear a small voice inside her making small but irritating comments. "So this is what it is to make love." She didn't feel significantly different. A little depressed, if anything. And the small voice murmured in a minor key, "Nothing has really changed, you know. Nothing is resolved." She felt she should get up, but the effort was more than she could manage. Time passed. She felt Gregory rising and shaking her lightly. "Anna, Anna, come on. I'll take you home. My parents will be back soon and that will spoil everything."

Anna opened her eyes and wordlessly raised herself to her feet.

She straightened her clothes, pulled the brush fiercely through her tangled hair. She felt Gregory watching her. He asked, "Are you all right?"

She nodded again, then looked him full in the eyes. "Gregory, Gregory — tomorrow we really must talk." Gregory glanced away. "Ya, sure, sure." Seeing her expression, he put his arm around her reassuringly. "Yes. Yes."

She decided to walk home alone. It would give her a chance to compose herself for her parents, in case they were already home. At the door, Gregory asked her if she'd like some ups in case she felt depressed tomorrow morning. Anna shrugged mentally and shook her head. Gregory squeezed her hand and gave her a quick kiss. Then she was on her own. She wasn't sure if today was a beginning or an end.

Anna turned the key in the lock. She had taken a long walk home. Thoughts of Gregory, of Cindy, of whether she might be pregnant ran through her mind. She told herself she was being silly. She *couldn't* be pregnant, not after one time. But she really must get hold of some contraceptives. She hoped there was no one at home. She didn't think she could face parental accusations right now.

Her parents' voices echoed angrily through the house. Should she let them know she could hear them? She heard her name mentioned in loud tones, so they were arguing about her. She stopped to listen.

"Sid, this girl is going to drive me crazy. Now she doesn't even come home after school. You must speak to her and lay down the law. We never had this trouble with Robert. [Anna's older brother, Robert, was away at college now.] Who knows what kind of people she's running around with?"

"Look, Norma. She's a girl, right? It's your job to talk to her. And you had better do it quickly."

Anna tiptoed back to the door, opened it softly, and closed it with a loud bang. She couldn't stand having her parents talk about her in that way. As if she were some strange problem child.

"Anna, is that you?" called her mother. "You mustn't slam the door that way. Come in here and have supper with us for once." Anna steeled herself for combat. Her mother seemed to forget that it was she who was never home in time to cook dinner.

"Anna, where have you been?"

Anna took her coat off and answered sullenly, "with a friend."

"Don't talk to your mother in that tone of voice," her father interjected.

Anna wanted to snap back but stopped herself and sat down silently. The three looked at each other for a long minute, uncomfortably, tensely, like rivals in a sparring match. Then her father, clearing his throat, began . . .

"Anna, I've been reading in the paper here that a lot of high school kids are taking drugs. Now I don't want you to get mixed up with these kids, you hear? Drugs are dangerous, not to be tampered with by children."

Anna shrugged her shoulders and gazed at the meat on her plate. The piece of dead flesh made her feel a little ill. She glanced up at her father. He had turned on his lecturing tone, and she turned off. It was amazing how naive her parents were. Children . . . She wondered if she still qualified as a child after today. Something urged her to play a bold card.

"Dad . . . Dad. Look, I've smoked marijuana, so don't lecture at me. It's nothing, see. Just makes you feel good, relaxed, like all those tranquilizers you take, see." (She heard herself mouthing Gregory's words and it shocked her a little. Just a few hours ago, she had been arguing on the other side. Her parents really made her act perversely, but they were so stupid sometimes. Talking about things they knew nothing about.) She heard her mother gasp. "You see, Sid, it's those hippies she's running around with."

She had been expecting this. "Mother, will you please define 'hippie' for me. What's a hippie? Am I a hippie? Because I don't wear the posh clothes you buy me and because I've smoked some grass. Imagine, your precious daughter a hippie!"

Anna's mother looked at her in dismay. "Anna, how can you talk to me this way?" She shed a few tears. "I'm your mother. I love you."

Anna felt the perennial guilt rising in her — but she pursued her tactic. "If you love me so much, how can you call my friends 'hippies,' as if that were a dirty word? You don't even know what goes on in my life and most of the time you don't care." She turned on her father. "And here you are lecturing about drugs. Have you ever used marijuana? Do you know what it's like? I know what's dangerous and what's not. I'm not a kid any more." She felt the tears rising in her eyes and she looked down at her plate.

Her father looked at her as if she were some alien being who had suddenly sprung into the midst of his household. "Who, tell me who gave you drugs? Was it that long-haired friend of yours, this friend we never see? Tell me his name and I'll phone him right now. I'll speak to his father."

"Leave her alone, Sid. I'll talk to her. We don't have to bring anyone else into this. I don't believe Anna's really taking drugs. Maybe she's just tried something once."

Her mother, assuming her tactful bridge-game tone, said, "Anna, you know we worry about you. We don't want you to get into trouble. Look at your cousin Nancy. She's a bright girl. She gets good marks in school. Why don't you go around with her friends? I'm sure they're not hipp . . . " Her mother stopped herself in mid-sentence. "I'm sure they're nice, interesting people. Your aunt is always telling us what a wonderful child she is and how nice her friends are."

Anna bristled. That Nancy again. And what did her mother know about Nancy except what her aunt chose to tell her. Sure that was what her mother wanted, someone to be proud of at bridge games. So that the neighbors would say what a good girl she was. She had heard the dear ladies talking in shocked voices of a neighbor's son who had been busted and spent a weekend in jail. The end of the world, the old gossips thought. Fodder for the bridge group.

Anna got up from the table. "Look, I don't want to talk about it. I can take care of myself. Don't worry, I won't spoil your good name."

She rushed from the room and threw herself on her bed, sobbing.

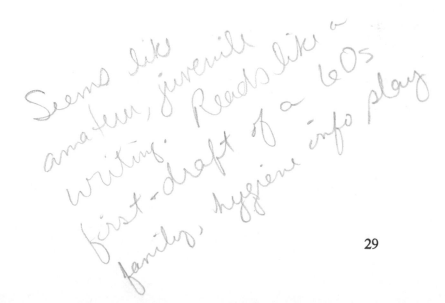

Seems like amateur, juvenile writing. Reads like a 60s first-draft of a family, hygiene info play

JEREMY

Perhaps another reason is that the elders lose knowledge of our heroes... Or they remember our heroes

J erry Blackstone. Jeremy Blackstone. Jeremy Arnold Blackstone. Jeremy sat printing all the variations of his name in bold capitals. No. It was not a particularly inspiring sight. He drew a line down the sheet of paper and in two neat columns listed a series of names:

Leon Trotsky   Albert Camus
Eldridge Cleaver   Pablo Picasso
Che Guevara   Feodor Dostoyevsky
Ho Chi Minh   Sigmund Freud
Thomas Paine

Men of action. Men of ideas, skill, genius. No, his name definitely did not have the right ring to it. Jeremy Blackstone: the first part had a worthy precedent, Bentham. But who thought of him now! And the second did contain "black" in it. That was something these days. Perhaps the names on his list had only acquired their peculiar resonance after these men had done their great deeds or written their books.

Jeremy stopped his daydreaming and returned to his book — a biography of Trotsky. He was fascinated by the way in which

31

Trotsky had been assassinated, so many years after he had ceased to have any active importance in the Soviet Union. Tortuously followed, tracked, through the alien landscape of Mexico; hunted down by Stalin's fanatical will. Stabbed innumerable times with a pick-axe by a petty agent in a dank room. The light gone from those piercing, fiery eyes. The internationalist fittingly buried in a foreign country. Jeremy wondered what his dying thoughts might have been. . . .

Dying. His thoughts reverted to Bob who had OD'ed a couple of weeks back. Bob was his age, only seventeen. The fact overwhelmed and frightened Jerry. And supposing it hadn't been a purely accidental death? Bob had been really down in these last few weeks, doing more and more drugs. He had talked wildly of the futility of existence, the destruction of the environment, the helplessness of the individual in a world controlled by a system of madmen manipulating powerful machines. And there was nothing Jeremy could say in return except to urge that those who felt as Bob did must band together and make their voices heard, put an end to the useless slaughter in Vietnam, in Biafra. . . . But Bob had merely answered, "So? So you paint a few more posters, you demonstrate a few more times. Eventually the fuzz kick your teeth in and the world goes on." Jeremy shook himself. He must stop turning this over and over in his mind. It *was* possible to do something. Something *had* to be done.

He looked at his watch. Nearly time for supper. Then the kids would be over for a meeting. They had to decide whether to demonstrate against the further incursions into Laos or not. Jeremy walked downstairs. The family was already seated in the dining room. His younger sisters were busy poking each other in the ribs and giggling over some unmentionable secret.

His father asked Jeremy to sit down. "Jeremy, I wanted to ask you something. I have a pile of campaign buttons here and I wanted to know if you and your friends would wear them. Perhaps some of you would even like to campaign for us?"

Jeremy gave his father a sour look. "Dad, I've told you before. We're not interested in that. We don't like your Democratic candidates any more than the Republicans. Not much difference between them anyhow. They just make promises to get votes."

"Look, Jeremy, I've had a little more experience in this world than you have. If you want this country to be run according to

He's waking up to the realities of the world.

your beliefs, then you have to support the candidate who's closest to these. Right? There's no other way. You can't just run around foaming at the mouth, complaining how bad things are, making impossible demands. That won't get you anywhere."

Jeremy wondered at his father's certainty, his complete assurance that the political system was functioning as it should, his inability to see its injustices.

"Dad, if I work for your candidate, right, and he makes certain promises, right — well, by the time he gets to Congress he's forgotten half of these, or he makes a deal with some other politician: 'I'll forget about this, help you in that, if you back me here.' Somewhere on the way to policy making, most of the issues are scrambled, turned upside down, and you end up having supported a man who's backing half of the wrong things."

"But that's politics, Jeremy. That's the way things work. You can't expect to build your dream world in two easy minutes. This is a democracy, after all. And it may take a little time to get things passed through the legislature, but at least you know that everyone's had a fair say in what's to be done."

"Ya. Sure. Democracy. 'Fair say.' Next you'll talk to me about justice and freedom. What about all the people who are getting killed while the White House is busy deliberating, talking? What about all the people who have no say, just because they're too poor or too black or too something? What about all the kids getting drafted? Can they say, 'No, I won't go to Vietnam. I won't kill helpless women and children?' Sure — if they want to spend a few years in jail. You can't just sit here and wait for the congressional machine to grind out its politics, all based on what's going to bring the most dollars home, anyhow."

"Jeremy, you're too young to understand these things. You have to see that reality isn't all black or all white. It's gray."

"Too young. Sure. Thank God, I'm too young. Too young to have produced the Second World War. Too young to have pushed the button at Hiroshima. But I'm not too young to go to Vietnam and murder a few people, am I? Your generation produced this disaster, this system of half-truths, of lies, of hypocrisy. You haven't been able to clear up the mess. You just get deeper into it. Now it's our turn to try to do something. And we'll do it our own way."

Jeremy's mother interrupted. "O.K., men. Time to eat. Politics is bad for the digestion." Jeremy and his father stared at each other until his father finally smiled, but Jeremy didn't reciprocate. Sure, it was easy for him to smile. These things weren't really serious for him. Life just went on whether thousands were killed or not. He remembered with distaste how yesterday his father had glibly lamented the past Biafran tragedy, the millions of starving people, while biting into a juicy steak. Jeremy had pushed his plate away. And his mother had innocently, perhaps slyly, commented, "But Jeremy. You won't help anyone by starving." These people were insensitive, immoral really. They took everything so lightly.

Now his mother asked him if he had gone by to see Bob's mother. Yes, he had. The poor woman was still in a state of semi-shock. She had had no idea that Bob was doing so many drugs, that he had been so depressed lately. It was amazing how people could live side by side, day by day, and still know so little about each other.

"I hope this teaches you and your friends once and for all that drugs are dangerous. Not to be played with." Jeremy's mother broke into his thoughts. "I know that people are beginning to say that marijuana is all right, but I still don't trust any of it. And once you get mixed up with that whole drug scene, you don't know where you'll end up."

"Sure, ma, sure. But you have to experiment with things before you can pass judgment on them. You can't just say everything's bad because the papers decide to play that angle one week. It's like saying a man's guilty before you give him a fair trial — if such things still exist."

Jeremy thought back on his experience with drugs. It wasn't a very extensive one in comparison to some of his friends, but he had tried everything from grass to heroin out of curiosity. He had to see for himself what all the talk was about, to feel what his friends were feeling. He liked grass, but for the most part he didn't feel it was worth his time. It was too energy consuming and ultimately he preferred having his head. There were too many things to think about, to be done, to spend time stoned or high. But he still ardently defended his right to take drugs in front of his parents. How could they judge what they hadn't experienced, just because something was illegal? Alcohol had been illegal for a time too, and it was certainly more dangerous than grass. He remembered reading somewhere that a vast number of deaths — was it 30,000? He wasn't sure — were caused by alcohol every year.

"Jeremy, I don't want you to experiment with things that can kill you. Is that clear?" Jeremy offered tacit agreement and excused himself. He didn't feel like arguing now and he was secure in the fact that he could handle the drug experience. That certainly wasn't his biggest problem for the moment. He wanted to prepare for the meeting. Tanya was supposed to be coming and he hoped she would make it. She had gradually been dropping out of the group and Jeremy missed her. Not only was she their best poster designer, but her acid hatred of everything in the establishment had spurred them on to more and more activity. Lately, however, she seemed to have lost interest. Not that her hatred for the system had diminished, but somehow she had resigned herself to a listless bitterness.

The doorbell rang. Jeremy stole a glance at himself in the mirror. He wasn't happy with his face. In his imagination, he measured himself against Trotsky. No, only the hair and glasses were the same. Perhaps a beard would improve things, but he doubted that the soft fuzz on his face would ever produce a bushy growth.

Footsteps were making their way up the stairs. He could distinguish the twins' voices, but there seemed to be a stranger as well. Jeremy went to greet them, wondering who it could be. The twins presented the visitor: a French cousin, André, who was in the country for a while and interested in radical movements. André had brought a portfolio of French posters dating from the May '68 uprisings. One by one, the others trickled in, Bruce, Eric, Doreen, and finally Tanya, looking pale, thinner, and visibly disturbed. Jeremy wanted to take her aside and talk to her, but it was impossible now that everyone was here.

The French posters were passed around and exclaimed over. André translated the captions in halting English. Perhaps they could make use of some of them. Jeremy was impressed by their sophistication, and particularly impressed by one. A large medicine bottle labelled: "Presse. Ne pas Avaler." "Press. Do not Swallow." Yes that would be useful here. They all had a good laugh over "Je suis Marxiste, tendence Groucho," a phrase which had been scrawled over a wall in Paris. "I am a Marxist, of the Groucho variety."

Then the business of the evening proceeded. Should they or should they not try to organize a school-wide demonstration next week? The twins reported that they had been asking around and it seemed that few kids were particularly interested. There was a definite flagging of interest this year. Everyone seemed to be regress-

[handwritten marginalia:] Wow What a stretch

35

ing into a state of lethargy. Jeremy noticed with dismay that Tanya was nodding her head in agreement. An image of Bob sprang up in his mind. The same resignation. He interceded.

"Well, if we can't arouse enough enthusiasm to get a demonstration going, we should at least pass out some information sheets on Laos. I've been doing some research, and if a few of you want to help, we could have it ready by next week." Bruce and the twins volunteered and André offered his assistance. The meeting dragged on. They discussed the pro's and con's of having a friend of Eric's older brother who had spent two years working in the south come to speak to a school audience. Jeremy found himself growing progressively more depressed. Something was wrong this year. No one seemed to have the same commitment as before. He wondered if he himself were losing faith in the group. Perhaps it was the presence of Tanya, looking so detached, so disinterested. He wished again that they could sit down and talk.

The meeting wound its way to a halt. Jeremy asked Tanya whether he could take her home. She agreed, but explained that she had moved away from home and was sharing an apartment with a couple of girls in the East Village. If he felt it was worth the long ride, she'd be happy to have his company. Jeremy nodded. He remembered that this summer Tanya had been having a lot of trouble with her mother, a pretty divorcée. Bob had told him that Tanya was seeing a black man fairly regularly and her mother objected strongly. Things must have come to a crisis, Jeremy thought, and perhaps they had both decided it was better for Tanya to move out for a while. He asked Tanya, hesitantly, what had happened. In a few abrupt phrases, she explained that she just couldn't take the scene at home any longer and had told her mother that if she wasn't officially permitted to move out, she would do so on her own in any case. Not wanting to lose her totally, her mother had agreed.

They got their coats and for a moment Jeremy thought he might ask his father if he could borrow the car. But he decided against it. It would just reinforce his father's oft-stated belief that in spite of all his radical ideas, he still needed the many comforts American life had to offer. The subway would do just as well, though Jeremy despised this claustrophobic underworld. Tanya was quiet, removed, after her short outburst. He thought that maybe she had changed her mind about being accompanied. He made some stilted com-

36

ments, about the weather, about the dirt in the streets, and was answered in monosyllables.

Once seated in the subway train, the need for conversation was thankfully drowned out by the piercing mechanical whoosh. Jeremy looked around him. He always felt imprisoned in the subway. No way out. Only these blank faces all around you, refusing to meet your eyes, refusing to be confronted. Yet there was this sense of unadmitted intimacy as you jostled your neighbor, and as the police strolled by on their rounds eyeing everyone suspiciously, a sudden sense of mutual hostility against this unspoken enemy. Jeremy caught Tanya's eye and smiled. She shrugged her shoulders as if to say, "Ya. The pigs. They're everywhere." A well-dressed woman, obviously a foreigner, stopped the cop and questioned him about something in a polite manner. He was noticeably taken aback, surprised by her smile, and uncomfortably he pointed to the subway plan. It came to Jeremy that the cop, too, must have sensed the hostility directed at him.

They came to their stop and made their way up the stairs. Jeremy was troubled by the idea that he would see Tanya home, meet her girl friends and still not have a chance to talk to her. He suggested a cup of coffee. Tanya nodded and led him to a shabby local coffee house. They ordered. Jeremy wondered how he might begin the conversation. He felt awkward faced by Tanya's silence, her distance. He steeled himself.

"Tanya, can you tell me what's wrong, what's bothering you? I'm worried about you." Tanya looked him full in the face. He suddenly felt she might burst out crying. She fumbled in her handbag, then asked him if he had a cigarette. He rose to get some from the machine in the corner. He handed her a pack and she lit up nervously, giving him a tremulous smile. "Thanks, Jeremy. You're nice." He waited. Tanya began, taking on a cynical tone he didn't like.

"So you want to know what's been happening in my life. Hmmm. It's true. I guess we haven't rapped for quite a while, and I've been avoiding the group. Only came tonight because I wanted to get out of the house." Her voice quivered. "It gets a little cold there, you know." She looked up at him, not knowing what to say next.

"Go on, Tanya. Tell me about it." Jeremy hoped he wasn't pushing her too hard, but he wanted to break her cynical tone. She stalled a little, then went on, still talking about herself as if she were someone else.

"Well, you know I was seeing Paul this summer and that's when the trouble with Mom reached its peak. We were hurling insults at each other like fishwives, day in, day out. Finally I moved out. I was pretty depressed," she continued. "I guess the constant arguing had taken a lot out of me. Paul was pretty comforting though. And we got along fairly well for a while. Then one day I woke up and realized he was making it with one of my roommates." Her voice broke. She lit another cigarette.

"Go on," Jeremy urged gently.

Taking a deep breath, Tanya began again. "Well, I guess I shouldn't have been jealous. You know, we were leading a pretty free existence and . . . But I *was* jealous, and I blew up. I told him all kinds of crazy things. That I had given up my home for him. That I would kill myself. I heaped it on him. Then I took a pile of pills. I didn't sleep or eat for a few days. Just kept taking ups. Felt awful. Paul stuck through it, not saying very much. When I had more or less come back to myself, he picked himself up one morning and told me it would be better if we didn't see each other any more. I haven't seen him since." Tanya stopped and fingered her hair nervously.

"Pretty rotten guy," Jeremy said.

Tanya rose to Paul's defense. "No, he wasn't. He just realized before I did that it was all over between us. I guess what had kept us together that long was my mother. Ironical, isn't it?" Tanya laughed. "We used to spend half our time talking about her unfairness, the prejudice of all these self-styled liberals." She laughed again, a little bitterly.

"Anyhow, I was pretty messed up for a while. That's why I didn't come to school much. I started doing the village scene." She hesitated. "Jeremy, I'm sure all of this sounds ridiculous to you. You're so positive, so eager to change society. Well, I'm finished with all that. It's pointless. There are so many things wrong with this world that the only way out will be when it blows itself up. Then whoever is left can start over again from the beginning."

Jeremy protested. "Tanya, you're beginning to sound like Bob. Please. I don't want you to end up that way."

Tanya shrugged. "I don't think I will, Jeremy." She looked at him seriously, as if asking for confirmation. "I've decided to go off to Vermont, to a commune."

Jeremy interrupted: "But that's copping out, Tanya."

38

"No it's not. I'm not getting anything out of school these days. I don't want to go to college. You know, I've been getting into myself a lot lately. With drugs and without. I think it's the only thing for me. I can live a quiet life. Paint. Get out of this filthy city. Be with people like me."

Jeremy protested again. "But Tanya, if everyone like you, with your brains, your abilities goes running off to the country, where will we be?"

"I told you, Jeremy. I don't think you're going to get anywhere by working against the system. That's the same as working within it. We have to change ourselves, before we change anything else. Learn how to live differently." Tanya seemed to be begging for confirmation. So Jeremy gave it.

"O.K., Tanya. I don't completely agree with you, but maybe for you it's the right thing. But don't give us up completely."

Tanya smiled. "I'll write you from Vermont. Maybe you can come up this summer."

Jeremy nodded. "Maybe."

They talked about some mutual friends, discussed what life would be like in the commune. But Jeremy felt depressed. First Bob and now, in a sense, Tanya. Both were lost to him. Maybe he was the one who was going the wrong way. He walked Tanya home listlessly. At the door, she gave him a quick kiss and squeezed his hand. "Thanks, Jeremy. I needed to talk. I feel a lot better now. And don't worry about me. I will write." Jeremy nodded and smiled. "Bye, Tanya."

He walked off. He passed a Chinese restaurant. The street in front of it was overflowing with rubbish. A guy, no older than himself, bearded and shabby, asked if he had some bread to spare. Jeremy fished in his pockets and dug out a dollar bill. "Wow, thanks man." He nodded and walked on. He heard the throbbing of a muted drum, a woman's shrill voice in the distance, yelling, "I'll get you man, I'll get you." Out of the corner of his eye, he glimpsed a shop window full of bright electric colors. Jimmy Hendrix's lost face stared out at him. He quickened his pace and broke into a run. He watched his fleeting image reflected in windows. No, he didn't look like Trotsky.

COMMENTARY

If there is a single impression that comes most strikingly to mind in looking at these composite profiles of contemporary teenagers, it is the extent and depth of their experience in the modern world. Today's adolescent cannot be kept under lock and key, sheltered from the shocks and complexities of existence in this nuclear age. The teenager will, even during junior high school years, come into contact with drugs, sex, the police, and perhaps death among friends. It is not our purpose here to lament or extol these facts, but to point them out so that parents can be fully aware of the environment in which their children live. Teenagers today confront what have traditionally, and perhaps not always correctly, been termed adult problems. And they, as well as their parents, must learn how to cope with these problems, and establish the point to which they can immerse themselves in this environment and still maintain a modicum of physical and psychological health.

Parents cannot prevent their children from participating in what have become typical adolescent activities. Experimentation with drugs, for example, seems to have become an intrinsic part of growing up. The parent who attempts to keep his child away from drugs is entering upon a pointless struggle. What is needed is a

41

realistic appraisal by all members of the family of the limits which must be set so that the teenager does not plunge into experiences which he cannot handle. Simultaneously, a sense of trust must be built up in the family, so that the youth can come home to discuss the difficulties he may be encountering; so that he can have some older, responsible person with whom to share his worries or troubles; if need be a shoulder to cry on without shame, without the feeling that individual strength is being jeopardized.

To the adolescent, matters which seem minor to the objective observer may take on gigantic proportions. Consequently the sense of having some basic form of support in the home, no matter what the dilemma, is extremely important. In the following commentary on the profiles of Anna and Jeremy we have isolated certain types of adolescent problems and their repercussions in the family, suggesting clues to possible ways of handling these problems.

Anna

Anna is in many ways representative of a large number of girls her age. She is worried about her dawning womanhood, slightly awkward in her new role. At times, she wishes she were a child again. But simultaneously, she resents her parents treating her as a child. She has a good fund of common sense, visible in her attitude to drugs, which she sees and uses as a form of recreation. Like most of her generation, Anna dislikes the restrictive school system which gives her little that is relevant to her own life. But when something catches her interest, speaks to her sensitivity, as does her English class, she reciprocates and does well. Like all people, young and old, she desires to be praised, to be paid attention to, and in this her English teacher as well as Gregory stand far above the parents who seem either to ignore her or put her down.

Anna's parents deny her basic individuality and her wish to be treated as a separate human being, an adult. As soon as Anna comes into breakfast, she is derided by her mother because of her appearance, chastized for a number of ills, and made to feel guilty for all the burdens she inflicts on her parents. This all-too-common parental tactic only serves to alienate the youngster from the parent. Though Anna may wish to talk to her mother, as a woman, about all the things which are worrying her, she knows that she will never be able to control her temper or resentment long enough to get over

42

the initial stage of a family encounter: accusation and endless questioning with no waiting for a response between questions.

If Anna's mother could enter a conversation without piling overt or intimated accusations on Anna and manifest a genuine interest in her life as a separate being, then Anna would have a responsible adult with whom to discuss her problems. However, this presupposes a willingness on the parent's part to grant the youngster some autonomy, some point of view which may differ from their own and still be valid.

There is one thing which parents are all too slow to realize. Children never turn out exactly as their parents had hoped or imagined, simply because they are individual beings. It is impossible to shape an individual fully in one's ideal image and though many parents never concretely define this ideal, children often sense it lurking in the background, some shadow against which they are always measured. This inflicts a sense of guilt on the child and decreases the self-esteem which is so necessary to him, especially during the difficult period of adolescence.

When Anna returns from her climactic afternoon with Gregory, her parents in no way sense that she is troubled. They cannot, of course, know that she has overheard their argument about her, but it can in no way help her relationship to them to realize that each one is shifting the responsibility of communicating with her on the other. Anna thus becomes an unwanted burden.

In their subsequent conversation about drugs, each of her parents employs a different tactic, one actually negating the other. Her father begins to lecture to her about the dangers of drug usage in inflammatory terms, a subject about which Anna knows far more. It is extremely dangerous for parents to attempt to teach their children when they know less about the subject than the youngster. This merely lessens their credibility with their child.

Anna, resenting her father's tone of lecturing as to an obstreperous child, loudly announces the fact that she has already had experience with drugs — perhaps in an attempt to shock her parents into giving her more attention, but more probably to make them realize that she is well on her way to being an adult. In this admission, she is stressing that she is a separate person who has experienced something that her parents have not and knows a good deal about this experience. Enflamed, her father reciprocates with threats rather than questioning her calmly on the nature and extent of her experimentation with drugs and setting some limits agreeable to both. His naïveté, his unreal appraisal of his daughter's situation has surprised Anna and certainly himself.

Anna's mother intercedes on her behalf, but for the wrong and again unrealistic reasons. She denies Anna's experience, pretends to herself that Anna is exaggerating, and goes on to give her examples of other children's good behavior. This further alienates Anna and she judges her mother's tears and claims of love to be at least partially false: a concern about her own pride and reputation, rather than Anna's immediate welfare. The mother's tactic denies the father's and leaves Anna with no one to turn to. On both sides, she is being asked to remain a manipulable child, something which her afternoon's experience, she feels, has ended once and for all. Anna is more troubled after the encounter with her parents than she was when she first came home.

In the last chapters of this book we have presented some model dialogues which provide hints on how to carry on a family conversation about drugs in precisely this kind of situation.

Anna's relationship with Gregory may strike parents as extreme for a girl of her age. However, if anything, Anna is an example of a careful city adolescent. She is not promiscuous by today's standards and her concern about Gregory's preoccupation with drugs marks her as a sensible, fairly mature person. Anna is seriously worried about the extent of Gregory's drug-taking. She half realizes that he is avoiding real problems as well as real relationships by immersing himself in drugs, and she tries to talk to him about this.

Gregory typifies what we, on our loose scale of drug usage, could call the recreational abuser. He is not really interested in anything outside the drug experience except perhaps women, though he pays lip service to "getting into oneself" — introspection. His one form of stimulation is drugs. He has almost dropped out of school; he is not motivated to do well at anything in particular; he is not really interested in social problems or doing anything about them, but like most of his generation, he feels deeply that all is not right with the world. Drugs for him are an extended form of recreation and recreation has usurped his entire range of activity. Without drugs he feels deadened, and he prefers to avoid troublesome issues rather than confront them, as his meeting with Anna reveals.

Although Gregory's parents are not portrayed here, they would be the kind of parents who do not take much of an interest in their

44

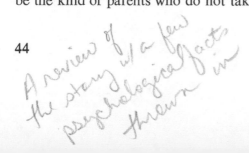

A review of a few of the story w/ a few psychological facts thrown in

child's life, apart from providing him with material benefits. He sees no reason to work, since his father does not seem to be particularly happy with his job and merely works to make a living.

Gregory, unlike Anna, is the youngster who could provide a serious problem, in that his indiscriminate use of drugs may lead him into dangerous territory — an accidental overdose, or more probably (since he knows drugs well and is not suicidal), a total unwillingness and inability to confront an adult existence. The only remedy for his situation is for either his parents, an interested adult, or perhaps a girlfriend like Anna, to give him a sense of the manifold possibilities of life. Gregory needs to find an interest in something outside drugs, to be rid of his philosophy of "I'm high, therefore I am." His problem is in many ways more directly a social one than a familial one. His environment, most immediately his schooling, has not provided him with a model of behavior outside the drug model, which could provide some kind of individual fulfillment.

Jeremy

Jeremy is a highly intelligent youngster who falls loosely into the category of the young radical. He represents a whole segment of American youth who feel that the political system in this country has failed and that the principles enshrined in the Declaration of Independence have been twisted so as to apply only to a small proportion of the population. These are youths with a strong social conscience, who question the American way of life, see its injustices, and apply a personal, but well-developed morality to all issues. Warfare is murder to them; Congress, the white-washed manipulator of a system of lies. The parents of these youngsters are generally fairly liberal in their views.

Jeremy is a rebel with a cause. He rejects the world created by his parents, denies that he is too young to have valid views, and works to institute that in which he believes. His relationship to his parents is a healthy one. This is not to say that he accepts his parents' decrees, but that the family is able to discuss issues together, and have an interchange of ideas and feelings without undue animosity.

What most parents fail to understand is that their adolescent children must rebel against them, if they are to grow into responsible adults. The rebellion does not have to be political as it is in Jeremy's

45

case, but can take many different forms: a refusal to accept parental strictures on dating, religious beliefs, or any number of things. The adolescent's need to create a separate identity necessitates that he set himself up as something different from his parents, an independent being. If parents try to prevent this rebellion by strict authoritative measures and succeed in doing so, they risk bringing up a child who will always in some ways remain a child. And though the parent may feel threatened or hurt by his teenager's rejection of all that he stands for, he must try to understand the youth's need to act in this way. Oscar Wilde has said that children begin by loving their parents. Then they judge them. Sometimes they forgive them. Adolescence is the period of judgment, and though the negative eye which youth casts on its forbearers may be very painful for each individual parent to bear, it is an essential part of the child's development into an autonomous human being.

Jeremy has tried all kinds of drugs out of curiosity, in order to satisfy his sense of experimentation. But he feels that they essentially do little for him. He prefers to have his mind clear to think about or discuss the problems which concern him most closely. However, he quickly defends his fellows' rights to use drugs, when his mother attacks this, since drugs, as he correctly intimates, represent one very clear sphere of rebellion by the young against the former generation. And as such Jeremy values them.

But Jeremy is worried and depressed by Tanya. He fears that her involvement in drugs is an escape from reality and activity, and her words remind him of Bob, his friend who suffered a drug-induced death. Tanya, and to some extent Bob, are representative of the youngsters who are overwhelmed by the personal and world problems their sensitivity and intelligence reveal to them. They are angry at everything, but cannot fully cope with their anger nor direct it into some form of positive activity. They, too, are rebels. Tanya, for example, has a relationship with a black boy, despite her mother's wishes. She moves away from home. But she is not quite ready to be totally independent and drugs provide her with a crutch, a way of escaping her depressions, a ready-made social group with a well-defined structure into which she can merge.

What can a parent troubled by a child like Tanya do? Very little. To threaten her with scare tactics, to try to force her away from drugs, will only push her farther into isolation and depression. The parent can only lend a sympathetic ear, suggest that there are

46

Insightful though at times simple

perhaps other ways of finding oneself than through drugs. For instance, Tanya is interested in something: her painting. Her mother could perhaps encourage her in her painting, make a special effort to share in this activity by going to galleries with her, in general let Tanya know that she has a contribution to make which is self-rewarding and fulfilling. In addition, Tanya has in the past been committed to social change; she is at present discouraged with the possibilities of having an impact on the problems of the society. With sensitivity to the adolescent sense of immediacy, the parent can reiterate that her participation in events is important and meaningful, and that social change comes only very slowly.

Right now, Tanya feels alienated from everyone outside her immediate drug environment. Therefore, she may be totally unable to accept what her mother tells her at this particular time. However, this does not mean that what is said will not help her at some future time. Often when people are at a crisis point they cannot really use a constructive statement, but the statement can act to set the stage for more adaptive thinking at a time in the future. At present, Tanya can only be treated gently, with sensitivity to what she is experiencing, so that her isolation does not increase. A supportive statement about her potential for making a contribution is a sensitive way of responding to her despair.

The idea of going to a commune, experiencing an alternate form of existence, may not be a thoroughly bad one in Tanya's case. And if she is made to feel that there are people who care for her on the outside, she will be able to make a choice, so that she will not feel forced into a path from which there is no return. Jeremy has quite naturally dealt with Tanya in the right way and it is a manner which parents could attempt to imitate.

To Tanya one can only say that the world needs her. If her political activity, like Jeremy's, seems to have no *immediate* impact, that does not mean that it is irrelevant and may not have a *cumulative* impact. It is adolescents like Tanya and Jeremy, with their strong moral consciences, who have forced questions on legislators that people might never have asked ten years ago. Their idealistic efforts are in no way useless.

In this chapter we have illustrated why there are few cases where drug usage is an activity unrelated to the totality of problems and experiences in an adolescent's life. Drug usage must be seen in perspective, as one of the manifestations of adolescent rebellion as well as a form of recreation. Generally, it is a mistake for the parent to call in the police, or unilaterally and precipitously to subject the child to unnecessary psychiatric examination if he finds his youngster using drugs. It is essential that the parent first try to understand what place drug-taking plays in his child's life. If, as in the cases of Anna and Jeremy, drugs are only one aspect of their teenager's recreational or rebellious activity, are taken fairly infrequently out of curiosity or in the same spirit as attending a movie, then scare tactics will only serve to produce more tension in the family. It is more important to consolidate family relationships, here, than attempt to coerce the youngster and thus alienate him further from the home.

However, if, as in the examples of Gregory and Tanya, drug-taking acquires a central place in the adolescent's life, more serious emphasis must be placed on it. Again, the central dilemma is not due to drugs; drugs merely make the problem evident to all. The tactic must again be one of trying to gain an understanding of why the youngster is taking so many drugs; pointing out to him in a reasonable fashion that the entirety of his life is being suffused by drug-taking, and that this could endanger his health and his future as well as his present. If parents do not feel that they can deal with this alone because they have no relationship with their child or the family situation has deteriorated to such an extent that communication is impossible, then there are services in schools and community centers where adolescents can go of their own accord to discuss matters with social workers, psychologists, or responsible adults.

Friends play an important role here. If an Anna can say to a Gregory, "There are other things in life besides drugs which deserve your attention," and argue her case forcefully, Gregory may indeed be turned on to other things: work with disadvantaged children, films, whatever the case may be. Or if Jeremy can convince Tanya that political activity does have some benefit or merely that he sympathizes with her, some good may come of it. There are no hard and fast rules in the spheres of human development or human relationships.

We have not gone into the matter of hard drugs here, though their use is becoming more widespread even among middle-class teenagers. *Heroin is an addictive drug* and the parent must explain to his youngster, or the teenager must recognize on his own, that he is physically endangering himself. The game of "I can beat the addiction," or "I can control it," is a gamble and the price is greater than money. Here, if the parent has no control over the child, and cannot arrive at some agreement with him, he must definitely seek outside help.

Pathological Drug Use

What we have described so far in these profiles are normal youngsters who may be having more or less difficulty in coping with their personal problems and their environment. Their use of drugs may extend into abuse, but it is in no direct way a sign of pathology.

However, there are youngsters whose abuse of drugs is an overt indication of deeply rooted disturbance, a disturbance which surpasses the usual difficulties and turmoils of adolescence. Drug use, here, may indeed intensify serious pathological problems. If a parent finds that his child is not only taking drugs frequently, but is also friendless, exhibits extreme changes of mood or acute depressions, is interested neither in school, outside activities, nor friends, and finds his only source of activity in drug-taking, then it is highly likely that his problems are pathological. At this point competent psychiatric and medical attention are needed.

The checklist is simple: a combination of regular drug use, friendlessness, lack of interest in all activities, and extreme moodiness do indicate an immediate need for outside help. But all these factors must be present simultaneously and parents must not jump to hasty conclusions. All adolescents are irritable, temperamental, and their shifts of mood must not be confused with pathology. Gregory, for example, uses drugs, lacks interest in most activities, but nevertheless has friends. This last factor is extremely important, for adolescents are naturally gregarious and oriented toward their peers. An adolescent with no friends whatsoever is probably suffering from some acute form of emotional disturbance.

We have tried to provide a personalized picture of adolescence and to sketch in something of the nature of the world the teenager inhabits. The complexity of the adolescent's life, the problems he encounters outside the home, his overriding need to be recognized as an individual being and for experimentation which may lead him away from the family and its particular values, are all things which parents too seldom choose to recognize. In the following chapter we shall present the opposite side of the coin; the adult world and the stresses it places on parenthood. This will permit the teenager to grasp some of the reasons behind his parent's actions and, hopefully, will reveal the parent to himself so that his role is placed into perspective.

PROFILES
OF THE
CONTEMPORARY
PARENT

DR. HENDERSON

Dr. Henderson let herself quietly into the house and shut the door behind her. Wearily she eased herself onto a large old-fashioned plush chair, slipped off her solid but worn working shoes, and began to rub her calves. She groaned, lit a cigarette, and tried to unwind. Yes, it was on days like this that she felt old, out-of-date, incapable of continuing her work.

Twenty years as a pediatrician with time out to raise two boys and now she was being criticized, openly defied by upstart interns, with their sleek long hair and ingenuous eyes. They disagreed with the strict, business-like way in which she confronted her young patients and their parents; her tone of distant assurance; her seemingly unfeeling attitude. Well, she wondered where their sloppy friendliness toward their patients would get them. After all, a doctor was there to treat disease, not play psychiatrist or priest.

Dr. Henderson shook her head. Perhaps she was getting too old, too impatient. The world had changed without her being totally aware of it. She had had to struggle as an intern, keep her nose close to the grindstone, work doubly hard to succeed since she was a woman in a man's world. She had accepted her parents' and teachers' values of what was right and wrong. She had modeled herself after her father — a country G.P. — and had never questioned her destiny. And she had married late, almost as an afterthought. Yes, perhaps the world had changed, passed her by while she was working and concentrating on other things. But on the other hand, there was little she respected in this modern world with its laxness, its lack of moral rectitude. Sloppy, undisciplined souls, that was it.

Dr. Henderson poured herself a glass of vermouth and sipped it slowly. Her husband would be home soon, probably even more worn out than she, and she wanted to greet him cheerfully. He had always slightly resented her preoccupation with work problems and so, many years ago, she had ceased bringing them up. It still annoyed him, after all this time, that she used her own name for professional purposes. She had originally decided that it would be unwise to use his name, after she had worked so hard to attain a reputation on her own. He had been happiest while the children were young and she stayed home to nurse them. Strange man, this Albert of hers. Still quite handsome, a little too stout perhaps. Sometimes she felt he was almost a stranger, though they had so many points in common. He too, had had to work his way up in the world, the business world. He seemed the typical self-made man: shrewd, abrupt, and a little pompous about his success these days.

Dr. Henderson thought of her older son, away at graduate school now. He had always been a great comfort to her, listening to her tales of hospital life with interest. She had been a little disappointed when he decided not to go to medical school, but that, after all, was his choice. Terry, her youngest son, was more of a problem. She sighed. Perhaps she was getting too old to cope with children. Terry, in his last year at high school, reminded her a little of the young interns at the hospital, with his hair a little longer than she would have liked. It was hard to talk to him, though she often wished she could do so. He always looked so troubled, as if the weight of the world were on his shoulders. Yet he was so shiftless, so undisciplined, always wandering around as if there were nothing constructive to do in this world.

He surprised her, this child of hers. How different he was from his brother, though it seemed to her that both had been brought up in the same way. She had always believed in being firm with children, making them do things around the house to help, setting limits on their dating, their use of the car, and so on. But Terry

54

had rebelled against this — not violently, mind you, but there was a certain tension, especially where his father was concerned. And of all things, he said he wanted to become an artist, and go to art school rather than college. It was absurd.

Dr. Henderson roused herself from her reverie. She heard her son's footsteps in the corridor. "Terry," she called, "I'm in here." Terry came in with his customary sullenness. She wanted to fondle him, but restrained herself. Still a child, she thought, but wanting to be a man.

"How are things, Terry? Did you have a good day at school?"

"Didn't go, this afternoon." Terry looked up at her, waiting for her reaction. She controlled herself.

"You didn't go? Why not, Terry? Are you ill?"

"No," he answered. "But I just didn't feel like it. Went to the flicks instead."

"But Terry, you can't just do something only when you feel like it. Why, if I didn't go into the hospital whenever I was in a bad mood, my patients would be in a sad state, wouldn't they?" She tried not to sound sententious. "In order to get anywhere we *all* have to do things in life that we don't particularly feel like doing."

"Now, Terry, I won't punish you this time, but promise me that you won't do this again. If for any reason you feel you can't go to school one day, come to me and we'll discuss it first. But no laziness around here. Is that understood?"

Terry nodded and she smiled. "O.K. Now go get ready for dinner."

Dr. Henderson edged her feet into her shoes and lifted herself slowly from the comfortable folds of her favorite chair. Terry was really a nice kid, but puzzling. She wondered what would become of him in life. He had so little sense of responsibility. It was a risky venture, this bringing children into the world. She thought of the countless children she had treated who had come into the world unwanted, and of the countless spoiled youngsters, whose parents looked at her with helpless eyes.

A loud slam shattered the silence of the house. Her husband's angry tones reached Dr. Henderson in the kitchen. Frightened, she dropped the cutlery and rushed to meet him.

"Where is that crazy son of ours?" he shouted. "Bring him to me this minute!"

55

"What's wrong, Albert? Tell me what's wrong."

"Just bring that kid to me, will you? If he weren't so big, I'd give him a good licking."

"Calm down, Albert, this is bad for your health." Dr. Henderson was worried. She hadn't seen her husband quite so upset for years. "What's Terry done? Tell me first."

"Calm down, you tell me. What's he done? That son of ours is a drug addict. That's what he's done. I tell you, I'm going to hand him over to the cops. Our son, a criminal."

Dr. Henderson just couldn't believe it. "Albert, how did you find this out? It can't be true. Not Terry." She felt herself go limp, helpless, like all the parents of those spoiled children. But surely, they hadn't spoiled Terry.

"Not Terry, she says. Just bring him to me. I met Mrs. Sharp at the bakery and gave her a lift home. You know that gay divorcée — used to work in the theatre — who's got a son Terry's age? Well, she tells me, as if it were nothing at all, that Terry was at a party at their place, and everyone was having a good time getting stoned. And she had the audacity to ask us to come over too, next time. That woman's mad, I tell you. Should be locked up with her son."

Dr. Henderson thought quickly. "Well, don't start yelling at Terry until after dinner. And ask him first. Maybe that woman's wrong." She was happy that she had been the first one to see her husband, before Terry. Otherwise he might have done something rash in his anger.

"I told you that son of ours was getting into trouble. He's crazy. Now he says he wants to be an artist!"

Dr. Henderson slipped out of the room to call Terry. She hoped her husband would calm down a bit, now that he had vented his first anger. All the old-world Italian came out in him at moments like this and it never solved anything. She prayed that he was wrong about Terry, but she didn't have the heart to ask him right now. He looked so unhappy these days.

Mother and son walked into the dining room together.

"So here comes my son, the drug addict. My son the artist. That's what I slaved all my life for, worked my way out of the slums for, so I could produce a drug addict, who paints pictures all day long. We taught you what was right and you turn into a drug addict. I swear, kid, if I ever catch you taking drugs, I'll call the

56

cops. For your own good . . ."

"Ah, Dad. Come on. You're being ridiculous. I'm no drug addict. So I did smoke grass a couple of times. So what? And no one asked you to slave all your life for me . . . "

"You see? You see? He even admits it. Ungrateful bum!" Dr. Henderson saw the veins bulging in her husband's forehead. He couldn't contain his rage. He was spluttering. Terry must really be kept under control. He was going too far. She interfered.

"Calm down, Albert. Eat your soup." She turned to Terry. "Terry, I'm a doctor. I know something about these things. Drugs are bad for you, dangerous, and your father and I are laying the law down now. No drugs. Is that understood?"

"Oh, Mom, everyone smokes marijuana. It doesn't do any harm. And besides . . . "

"You heard me, Terry. Now eat your soup."

Dr. Henderson saw Terry staring blankly into his plate as her husband slurped his last drops of soup noisily.

"Terry, believe me. We know what's good for you. So listen to us."

"Man, you people depress me. You're just getting senile. You don't understand what's happening in the world anymore."

"Did you hear that, Doctor? We're senile. Bite the hand that feeds you. We depress him. These crazy kids with their invisible ailments. Depressed? You know when you're depressed, Terry? When you're going around the streets hungry, looking for a piece of bread. That's when you're depressed. You should have lived during the depression. We had to work so hard to eat that we forgot about our suffering. You're just lazy. Crazy. Not depressed. If you had any will power, any guts, you wouldn't have these so-called problems of yours, that troubled face you drag around. My son, a drug addict, and an artist. If you want pictures, you buy them — when you have enough money to do so."

"Yeah, Dad. Sure. You know all about everything. You have deep feelings. Why I bet you never felt anything in your life."

Dr. Henderson shuddered, but managed to control her voice and say, "Terry, that's enough. You have no right to speak to your father that way. Go up to your room and I'll see you later. I don't want to hear another word now."

Terry strode out. She watched him go, unhappily. He didn't really mean all the things he had said against them, she thought. It was just his generation and their way of behaving. Yes, she was definitely getting old. If she couldn't handle Terry, then maybe the interns were right. Maybe her approach was wrong for this new world. She turned to her husband, who had slumped into silence now that Terry had left. She could sense that he was deeply hurt.

"Albert, these kids aren't like we were, you know. It's no use giving them examples from the past. They don't believe in the same things we did: in work, in getting somewhere in the world. Maybe we just spoiled Terry. Maybe it's the times. But you must take it easy. What can we do? We're getting old, you know."

"Yes, Doctor." Albert looked at her mournfully, much like a lost child himself. "I believe you're right. We're getting old."

THE BORDENS

Sunday breakfast in the Borden household was generally a happy affair. Mr. and Mrs. Borden, clothed in colorful robes, prepared dozens of pancakes for their three children: Judy, 10, Pat, 13, and Johnny, 17. The smell of crispy bacon mingled with the aroma of brewing coffee pervaded the house, and the sound of Mr. Borden's favorite records echoed in the background. Floppy, the Irish setter, observed the bustle with wise eyes.

This Sunday, however, there was a definite tension in the atmosphere. The pancakes were there, and so was the coffee; Floppy was sprawled in his usual corner. But the children had awakened to the angry voice of their mother shouting, "If you ever do anything like that again, I'm marching right into a lawyer's office and demanding a divorce. I won't stand for it. Imagine, a man of your age. Parading around with a black whore. I won't have it, I tell you . . . "

And their father responding, strained but calm:

"Stop being hysterical, Hannah. And stop exaggerating. Leave the blackness out of this. You should know better. And lower your voice. The children will hear you."

"They *should* hear me, hear about the adventures of their beloved father . . . "

At this point Johnny roused himself and clattered into the bathroom. He wanted his presence to be known, so that his parents would stop arguing. It hurt him when they went on like this. Patricia was already there, tears streaming down her face. He tried to comfort her, to tell her that it was probably all a misunderstanding. Their father had to see all kinds of people in his work and their mother was probably exaggerating. She often did.

Patricia dried her eyes and they both walked into the bright kitchen together, trying to pretend that nothing was wrong. Mrs. Borden took one look at Patricia and ran over to embrace her.

"Have you been crying, honey? Don't. I love you." Patricia struggled out of her grip and sullenly sat down at the table. Mrs. Borden turned to her husband and muttered, "You see? You've even turned the children against me."

The telephone rang, while Mr. Borden heaped pancakes onto the children's plates. Patricia ran to answer and bumped into a sleepy Judy making her way to the kitchen. It was one of Patricia's friends. There was a brief silence in the kitchen in which only Patricia's voice was heard. "Yes, Doreen. It's me. No . . . Did she really? . . . I think she's crazy. . . . Well, tell her to fuck off. . . . O.K. . . . I'll call you back later. Can't talk now. . . . Yeah . . . Bye."

As Patricia re-entered the kitchen, her mother lashed out at her: "Pat, I won't have you talking that way in front of your friends. I forbid you to utter obscenities in public. Is that understood?"

Patricia looked at her mother in surprise. This was too ridiculous. "But, Mom, you've heard me talk that way before. What's this sudden change? You're a hypocrite. You . . ."

"I don't care, Pat. I won't have it. What happens in the home is one thing. How you speak in front of other people is something else."

Mr. Borden cleared his throat to draw attention to himself and passed some syrup around. He passed his hand through his thick gray-streaked hair. The day had gotten off to a bad start and the children were upset. He tried to introduce a topic which would interest everyone and ease the atmosphere. They always liked to hear stories of his work in juvenile court, so he told them of a case which had just come up yesterday. A fourteen-year-old black boy from a ghetto area had been caught in possession of a cache of drugs. He claimed that he had not known what was in the cache, but was merely delivering it for his older brother to another area of town. He also described in vivid detail how the cops had kicked him in the groin, shoved him into the police car, and treated him in a generally brutal fashion. Mr. Borden had offered to defend the boy without taking any fee, though he didn't totally believe in his innocence about what he was carrying. Still, he thought that time in a reformatory would do the boy more harm than good. Now, Mr. Borden presented the case to the family and asked them how they would handle it if they were the judges.

Johnny immediately exclaimed that it was the cops who should be on trial, not the boy. They had no right going around beating people up. If the cops were tried as often as people handling drugs, he argued, the country would be in a much better state.

"But, Johnny, that's not the point here," Mr. Borden replied. "Granted that the police sometimes abuse their rights, but you have to remember that they often deal with hardened criminals, who would only too happily treat them in the same way. The boy did have quite a large amount of drugs on him, and the law says that this is a serious offense. Now, should he be allowed to go totally free?"

"Yes, Dad. Of course he should. Even you've said that the laws on drugs are too severe. And the kid didn't even know what he was carrying."

"That's only what he claims, Johnny. We have no proof." Johnny shrugged at his father and at the injustice of the law.

"What if that kid had been me, Dad? Would you still say the same thing?"

"Of course, Johnny," Mr. Borden replied. "If you had broken the law, I would have to question all the possibilities of your guilt or innocence. But I hope you never get yourself into that kind of situation. I think we've talked about it enough for you to know better, and I've explained to you that there are non-chemical ways of turning on — tutoring kids in the ghetto, music, walks in the country, for example." Mr. Borden gave Johnny a look of mingled severity and friendly advice.

"You'd allow your own son to be arrested?" Mrs. Borden queried accusingly. "Don't worry, Johnny, I'd protect you." She threw her husband a challenging look.

Mr. Borden chose not to reply to his wife's comment. He realized that she was attacking him, not really pondering the implications of her statement. He turned to his daughters.

"How would you judge this case, Pat?"

"I agree with Johnny."

"Me too," echoed Judy.

"What about you, Hannah?"

Mrs. Borden looked at her husband with veiled envy. How was it that he was always able to involve the children in reasonable conversation, while her efforts at talk were generally answered with hostility? And yet she felt he was a blatant enemy to the family they had set up together. She wondered whether the gossip she had heard of his doings was correct, and her thoughts turned to jealousy.

She caught herself, and made an effort to think of the matter at hand. It was no use getting worked up in front of the kids. Her immediate reaction to the case her husband had presented had been to say, "Lock the boy up." After all, it was his kind who might, quite unwittingly, put her own children into precarious situations. It was well and good for the kids to sympathize with the boy, but they had no idea of the danger he might represent — even indirectly — to themselves. She sensed the children looking at her, waiting for her opinion, and she felt helpless. If she uttered what she believed was right, they would only turn against her. She shrugged, and in a small voice said, "I don't know. I don't know."

"Oh, come on, Mom," Pat rebuked her. "A judge can't say he doesn't know."

"That's right," Judy echoed.

"All right then," Mrs. Borden acquiesced. "Let him go."

"That's the spirit, Mom," Johnny encouraged her. "That's the spirit."

The children looked expectantly at their father.

"Well then, I partially disagree with all of you," Mr. Borden commented. "The boy can't be allowed to go scot-free. He may get the idea that peddling drugs is all right, as long as you come up with a good excuse. And we can't allow that. You know how many kids in New York City alone have died because of drug use. And this boy has committed an offense. Ignorance is no excuse before the law. Still, he's young and harsh punishment would probably only embitter him, make him into an angry social outcast. So we might give him a suspended sentence and place him on probation, together with a strict warning to stay away from the whole drug scene."

"Yeah, Dad, you're probably right," the children nodded.

Mrs. Borden wondered at her husband. Here he had said everything that she had been afraid to say and the children still looked up to him. Maybe it was because he didn't spend quite so much time with them as she did. Maybe it was the good stories he came up with. She really didn't know, but somehow she felt herself abused from all sides. Tears welled in her eyes and she tried to stop them in a rush of activity. With brittle cheerfulness she asked, "More food, anyone?" and brought a tray of hot muffins to the table. Her husband caught her eye and smiled. Well, maybe she was being a little too harsh with him. Her nerves had been on edge lately. She suddenly found herself with too much time on her hands now that the children were growing up. Perhaps she should get herself a part-time job.

It occurred to her that since the issue of drugs had been brought up, it might be a good time to question Pat about her new friends in junior high. She had some qualms about this outspoken daughter of hers who had suddenly been transformed from a playful tomboy into an arrogant young woman.

"Pat, who is this new friend of yours, Doreen? Why don't you ever bring her home?" she began, attempting to sound casual.

"A girl," Pat answered curtly.

Mrs. Borden felt her anger rising. Pat was becoming impossible. "Pat, don't speak to me in that cocksure fashion. I'm your mother, remember?"

"Oh, tell her," Johnny insisted. "She won't mind."

"O.K.," Pat said, shrugging her shoulders. She looked up at her mother defiantly. "A black girl, who has a nice black brother."

"That's not a description of a person," Mrs. Borden heard herself saying defensively.

"But, Mom, I heard you telling Dad before . . . "

"That's enough, Patricia!" Mrs. Borden exclaimed as she barely managed to leave the room without bursting into tears. Yes, everyone was against her today. She heard her husband explaining, "Your mother's tired. She didn't sleep very well last night. You should be kinder to her."

"Oh, Dad. She's always making such a fuss — asking so many silly questions."

"But dear, she's worried about you. It's natural. You're growing up now and she feels she's losing you. Can you understand that?"

Patricia muttered an acknowledgment.

"Now all of you, scat to your rooms. I want to talk to your mother."

Mr. Borden went to join his wife. Yes, she was being difficult these days. Kids were quick to pick that up, but not so quick to forgive. He realized that it was more than partially his fault. Yet he wished that the kids didn't have to be caught in the midst of it. He saw his wife's tear-stained face and put his arm around her.

"The children hate me now," she blurted.

"No they don't, honey," he consoled her. "No they don't. You're just being too sensitive. You have to stand up to them. Say what you think openly. Come on, calm down now. I'll take you out to dinner tonight."

Mrs. Borden took a deep breath to control her sobs and looked into her husband's eyes. Yes, perhaps he was right. Things would straighten themselves out tomorrow. At least she hoped so.

THE ROJACKS

"Anthony, Anthony. Where are you? Come and get your allowance," Mrs. Rojack called up the stairs. She waited for a response, but she heard only the echo of her own voice, distantly muffled. The house was strangely silent. She sighed and went to sit in her study. There was still a lot of work to be done this evening and she had no time to waste. The case histories had to be studied before tomorrow morning's meeting, as well as the mammoth folder containing the clippings on child abuse. Really, that Anthony was becoming a nuisance. Sometimes she wondered why she had ever had a child. Social pressure probably. The myth of the sterile, childless woman. But all that was changing now, thank God. Women could admit they didn't want children and still not outrage their neighbors' conventional sensibilities. Contraception was now considered a matter of course. Perhaps she had just been ahead of her time.

Still, here she was with Anthony. A nice kid, all things considered — good-looking, with his father's large blue eyes, but constantly nagging at her, pretending to have world-shattering problems. Why, he should look at these case histories of abused youngsters and what they had to put up with: alcoholic parents, countless beat-

65

ings, poverty. It was really outrageous. And here was Anthony, complaining, though he had everything he could possibly want, plus limitless possibilities of education, career, travel. Mrs. Rojack glanced at her watch. Seven o'clock. Her husband must be working late again. That meant that she had a good three hours ahead of her to go through all the material. She settled down at her desk and immersed herself in her papers.

Suddenly, she felt a presence behind her. She wasn't sure how much time had elapsed. A pair of eyes bored into her back, with what she felt to be hostility. She was almost afraid to turn around. Ridiculous! She laughed at herself. No one could have come into the house without her hearing. It must be the effect of reading these near-sensationalist case histories. She glanced over her shoulder, then turned her chair fully around. There stood Anthony, looking like the spectre of a melodrama — hair tumbled, shirt askew, eyes staring and bloodshot, cheeks pale, and the deep crease of a frown in his forehead. She didn't know whether to proffer some aspirins or laugh out loud, but controlled both impulses.

"Anthony, really. You should make your presence known when you walk into a room. Stalking in like that, you almost scared me half to death. Where were you when I called you? Didn't you hear me?"

Anthony looked at her with blank eyes. "I don't feel well. I was sick — puking in the bathroom. I don't know what's wrong with me. I've got this terrible pain in the stomach." Anthony looked mournfully down at the general area where his stomach lay, passed his hand over it, doubled over as if he were in the midst of a painful cramp, and sat down on the nearest chair.

"Oh, Anthony. Stop exaggerating. We don't need histrionics around here. You've probably just eaten something that doesn't agree with you. So make yourself a glass of hot milk. I'm very busy tonight." Mrs. Rojack gestured at the pile of papers on her desk.

Anthony sat there, unwilling to move, and looked up at his mother. "Maybe it's because I took these pills," he mumbled.

Mrs. Rojack restrained her rising frustration. Always dramatic, this son of hers. "What kind of pills, Anthony?" she asked.

"Oh, just pills," he muttered and doubled over again.

"Well, do you want me to call the doctor?" she queried, her mind already on her work.

66

Anthony shook his head. "All right, then," Mrs. Rojack responded. "Why don't you go lie down for a bit. You'll be better in the morning." Anthony didn't move. "Very well then, you can sit here with me. There are some magazines on the table."

Mrs. Rojack returned to her work. She thought that perhaps she should pursue the question of what kind of pills Anthony had taken. But she was half afraid to do so. He was old enough to be reasonable about what he swallowed and she had, long ago, bought him a drug handbook to inform him of what was permissible and what wasn't. And she didn't want to get into an involved conversation on the pros and cons of drug-taking. It was enough that as a social worker she was questioned about these things all day. Mrs. Rojack began to make some notes from her files. Then she felt Anthony looking over her shoulder.

"What are you doing, Mom?" he asked. She sighed. He really was determined to disturb her this evening. She would never get her work finished and it was essential that she brush up on these cases.

"We're having a meeting on child abuse tomorrow and I'm going over some notes," she explained, trying to be patient.

"Oh yeah?" Anthony said skeptically. "What do you do with these kids?"

"Well, first of all, we're trying to isolate which cases are most in need of help and determine what kind of help is of primary importance: medical, economic, or psychiatric."

"What good does that do?" Anthony demanded. "You only end up helping — if you can call it that — ten or twenty or at the most thirty kids. You should be spending your time working out a way of changing the system, so that these cases of abuse never arise. And that means," Anthony raised his voice and looked at her defiantly, "that you have to overthrow the present system. You're just a cog in the wheel, Mom. Just helping to perpetuate injustice."

Mrs. Rojack trembled a little. How obnoxious he could be at times! "I see your stomachache is gone," she rallied.

Anthony turned away. "Look, Anthony. I'm a social worker, not a politician. I do my work and I think it's worthwhile. Now go and listen to some music or something. We bought you that expensive stereo set for Christmas. You might as well get some use out of it."

"Don't feel like it," Anthony muttered.

"All right," Mrs. Rojack responded, turning back to her desk.

"But I have to work." She could hear Anthony settling into the chair and leafing through a magazine. She hoped he would leave her alone for a while. It was already past nine.

Anthony sat turning the pages and looking at his mother's stiff back, the thin neck rising into a bun of auburn-gray hair. His mother, from the back, looked just like a spinster he had read about in a Victorian novel. He wondered if she ever experienced anything deeply in her life; ever really loved his father or felt anything for those people she was endlessly working with. Well, maybe social workers were trained not to feel anything. It was a pointless life she led, in his opinion. He rose to go, but changed his mind.

"Mother," he drawled, enunciating each syllable of the word, baiting her. "Moth-er." Mrs. Rojack turned toward him absent-mindedly. "Mmmm?"

"Have you ever worked with kids who refuse to go to school?"

"Yes, a little," she replied half-heartedly.

"Well, what do you do with them?"

Mrs. Rojack searched into her past experience. "First you try to find out why they're playing truant. Then you try to make them see why it's essential for them to go to school, how it will affect their future. You try to find out what they're interested in doing later in life and you show them what steps they have to follow to achieve it."

Anthony stood up and paced abruptly across the room. He ran his fingers through his length of dark hair. Then, looking down at his mother, he announced, "Well, Mom. It looks as if you have a case on your hands. I haven't been to school in a week and I have absolutely no desire to go next week or the next." His voice trailed off and he slumped into his chair.

"Anthony," Mrs. Rojack muttered in disbelief. "That can't be. Why you've always been such a good student. We've never had any problem with you because of that."

"Well, you've got one now," Anthony muttered. He stood up nervously and began pacing again.

Mrs. Rojack looked at her son in dismay. "Anthony, you're being silly, childish. What will your father say?"

"I don't give a shit what he says! He'll be too busy to worry about it anyhow. I'm surprised you've even got the time to turn around from your desk."

"Anthony, that's unfair. Your father and I have always given you everything you've wanted. You know that. Why just last week . . . "

"Sure, Mom, sure. But you still haven't settled my case, Madame Social Worker." Anthony looked at her disdainfully. "What about my truancy problem?"

"Well, I never! Anthony, be reasonable. You know you have to go to school. You're becoming impossible lately, always complaining, or sick. I think maybe we should send you away for a while, for a change of scene. How would you like to spend a term in a school in England? It would be interesting and might do you good."

"Do you good, too." Anthony mimicked her. "Sure, why don't you send me away? I won't even bother you with letters. How about shipping me off to Vietnam? That would be even better. They can send me back in a wooden box. Then this particular case will be closed for good. How about that?" Anthony gave her a glance full of hatred and rushed out of the room.

"Anthony, Anthony. Come back here. That's not what I meant." Mrs. Rojack rushed after her son. She heard him saying, "Next time I take pills, I'll make sure I take enough of them." Then he slammed his bedroom door.

Mrs. Rojack retreated. She felt a little frightened. Anthony was behaving so strangely and it wasn't like him to make suicidal threats. She wondered if perhaps they hadn't been neglecting him too much, assuming that now that he was sixteen, he could manage fairly well on his own. But there was all her work and her husband's. Anthony should be able to understand.

She heard the garage door opening. Mr. Rojack entered, chewing at a large cigar. "Hello, dear." He gave her a dry peck on the forehead. "God, I'm tired. My eyes are crawling out of my head. That drive home gets longer every day. Think I'll just take a shower and jump into bed."

"But, Mark. I wanted to talk to you about Anthony. He's in a terrible state today."

"Oh, he'll hold until tomorrow morning, honey. I couldn't keep my eyes open long enough to make one intelligent comment. Good night." He gave her another peck and walked off to his room.

Mrs. Rojack stared despairingly after him. Then she shrugged and turned back to her desk.

COMMENTARY

Just as parents very often fail to recognize that their children lead complex individual lives, teenagers also frequently fail to understand that their parents exist as separate beings who have to contend with the pressures of their personal lives or of the business or professional worlds which may infringe on their role as parents. The harried father, troubled by business pressures or professional responsibility, may not have the time or peace of mind to pay sufficient attention to a demanding adolescent. Similarly, a mother caught up in personal, emotional difficulties or problems related to work, may take her children's development for granted and only realize that something has gone wrong when a crisis arises. The family unit is, after all, only *one* sphere of interpersonal relations. Since parents and children tend to see each other only in family situations, it is difficult for them to realize that each separate individual in the family leads a different life outside the family. But this is a fact which must be remembered time and again, if parents and children are to arrive at any kind of understanding, for the sphere of activity outside the family necessarily intrudes upon and influences the moods, worries, and problems within each family situation.

In most families, so little sharing of the problems related to these extra-familial roles takes place that the adolescent who sees his father in his professional capacity for the first time is often astounded. Likewise, the teenager who is dissatisfied with a narrow-minded parent is frequently surprised when a friend finds his mother an understanding individual with whom he is capable of discussing many difficulties. This is because the family unit generally only allows its members a one-sided view of each other — a view that is fraught with the tensions of constant cohabitation. If understanding and beneficial communication is to come about in a family, it is essential that each of its members attempt to see the others in a three-dimensional manner, as beings who exist in both closeness and distance, as parents and children as well as members of a larger community or profession, and as individuals who are marked by the experience which takes place outside the household. Thus, there is, in the family, a necessity for a sharing of the experiences, adventures, and worries related to the external world. And as we see in the profiles in this chapter, this kind of sharing very rarely takes place.

Teenagers also often fail to realize that their parents are genuinely worried about them and, from what their experience has taught them, with good reason. Frequently parents are not merely panicking unnecessarily. The world they live in has made them see that responsibilities are many and the ability to respond to them is of central importance; that self-discipline, the ability to work consistently at something, is more frequently rewarded than self-indulgence — what the youth cult calls "hanging loose." Though they may not totally disagree with or disapprove of the "now" generation, their experience of reality has taught most adults that the ethics of this generation — which we discuss in the following chapter — are not those which will ensure success in the world. Even though the teenager may reject his parents' values, it is necessary that he recognize that his parents are concerned for his future and that, on the basis of their own experience, they more often than not have something that they can teach him: whether it be something as wide-ranging as the workings of the legal system, their activities in the war or the depression, or merely how to fix a car engine.

The difficulties of the adolescent phase have been ennumerated time and again. The teenager, with a growing awareness of the world around him and the aggressive demands of his own developing individuality, is confronted by a series of personal and psychological problems which are so intense that they tend to make him largely interested in himself and his own reactions, rather than in the people around him. Generally, people are important to him only insofar as they make him feel various things — guilt, irritation, hostility, pleasure. The basic narcissism of this stage of life results in an acute sensitivity on the teenager's part, but a sensitivity which is only directed toward himself. Thus the teenager may often be unaware of his cruelty or insensitivity to his parents. But it is a very real cruelty.

The teenager who rejects his parents' values, and aggressively insists that his parents are obsolete, generally does not realize how much pain this can cause his parents. To be rejected by someone who has grown out of one's own flesh and blood, someone who is immeasurably close to one, is tantamount to annihilation. Every time a teenager proclaims to his parents that they are out-of-date, and rejects their major views, he is denying them the totality of their lives, all that they have experienced. This is intensified by the fact that in America the young are the focus of public attention, the subject of the media's gaze. In a country where the emphasis is on the future rather than the past, the young are the embodiments of that future and in many ways the arbiters of future values. Thus the parents' existence is threatened from all sides.

In the deeper reaches of the parental psyche, there is always some regret and anxiety about the child's growing up. As the child develops into an adult, the parent is confronted by his growing irrelevance to the central sphere of human activity, and by his own imminent death. The parent is being replaced. This is why parents so often wish to keep their children just that, and often, even after their children have long been recognized as adults by the external world, they continue to treat them as ten-year-olds. It is painful to see one's child mature into an adult, to be rejected by him, and finally to be replaced; and this pain is something which the teenager should take into consideration before he cruelly insists that his parents are obsolete.

It is also the adolescent's responsibility, rarely met, to explain himself and his concerns to his parents. All too often, teenagers simply give up on their parents and judge them to be totally incapable of understanding anything. It is important that the efforts at mutual education about mores and values never be abandoned, no matter how difficult this task may seem. A parent who may not be able to hear something in one mood may be more receptive in another. It is the teenager's job to make himself understood. In the subsequent analysis of the three parental profiles in this chapter, we shall examine the positive and negative aspects of certain kinds of parents and the ways in which they react to various family situations.

Dr. Henderson

In the Henderson profile, we find what could be called an example of the authoritarian parent. Both Dr. Henderson and her husband have a well-defined sense of what is right and what is wrong; and they have no qualms about attempting to impose these values on their son. Dr. Henderson is firm in her way of viewing the world, strong-minded but not rigid. She has always led her life in a disciplined, positive manner, as if she had a definite goal in view. However, though she is against the youth culture and what she calls its "laxness, its sloppiness of soul," she does question her own mode of thinking and being in relation to it and feels herself to be slightly old-fashioned. This is evident in her thoughts about the interns at the hospital as well as her approach to Terry.

She is firm in her disapproval of Terry's absence from school in order to go to the movies, and she tries to explain to him, in a reasonable manner, that in life one must often do what seems unpleasurable in order to reap later benefits. Terry may not agree with her view, but at least he has had the benefit of a reasonable explanation, not a hostile over-reaction to what he has done.

Similarly, Dr. Henderson does not say that he must not, above all, be an artist, nor does she mock his desire, although it goes against the grain of what she personally might wish for her son. She recognizes that he is troubled and that it is a function of his age as well as his generation. Her reaction to her husband's loud accusation of Terry's drug-taking is to reason with her son in a calm manner and explain that she, as a doctor, as an authority, knows that drugs are dangerous, and therefore she forbids him to take them. Terry may not follow her orders, but he knows where his parents stand on the subject and why this is their view. Dr. Henderson has acted in an appropriate manner and one can imagine that her son has sufficient respect for her to take her view into consideration.

Dr. Henderson is a positive example of the authoritative parent who is a strict disciplinarian and demands respect rather than friendship from her children. When Terry calls his father ridiculous and insults him, then terms both his parents senile, she orders him, in a controlled manner, to leave the room. And Terry obeys. Dr. Henderson's style of treating her children is one which is not held in high esteem now, nor regarded as the model of parental behavior, perhaps because anything to do with authoritarian action is suspect. However, to be authoritative, to be strict with children, is not always to be authoritarian in the bad sense, and Dr. Henderson's manner of dealing with Terry cannot be thoughtlessly criticized. She is fair, though stern, and generally tries not to allow her own tiredness and dissatisfaction with her work to interfere with her attitude toward Terry. And she is consistent in her way of dealing with him, controlled and reasonable in most respects.

In our experience, there is one danger in this particular parental model, especially if the parent has a strong, almost over-riding personality. The danger lies in the possibility of the parent destroying the child's own individuality and crushing him totally by the very force of his firm stand. The authoritative parent can be over-protective and thus trap the youngster in childhood by inhibiting his growth away from the home and family and his experimentation in the external world. The parent may be so strong that the maturing youngster, with his still delicate individuality, may be overwhelmed, and may retreat into being merely a lifeless duplicate of the parent — a mouthpiece for his parent's ideas and views. The authoritarian parent must take stock of his own position and try to judge fairly if he is crushing his child: that is, being overly powerful, rather than simply firm. Terry, for example, has certainly not been crushed, and Dr. Henderson typifies the firm parent.

Dr. Henderson's husband's case is slightly different. He is totally authoritarian rather than authoritative, and there is a good deal of uncontrolled irrationality in his behavior toward Terry. He insists that Terry is always in the wrong, while he, the father, knows all the answers. He mocks Terry's desire to be an artist, unreasonably links it to drug-addiction, and refuses to realize that his son may be suffering in his own way. Dr. Henderson's husband is what one could call the "pre-psychological" kind of parent — the one who denies that there is any form of psychological pain. If Terry is depressed, his father sees not depression but laziness, and a little will-power is his answer to "all that." He does not recognize that there can be a reason for Terry's feelings, nor even that they *are* real feelings. Only *hunger* is suffering. He is totally unwilling to see things from his son's point of view, and even to try to understand or discuss the context in which his son's actions take place. He is not firm, but rigid in his values.

Thus, he over-reacts when he hears that Terry has been taking drugs and threatens him with the police. His attitude and his basic self-righteousness about this can only oppress Terry totally, or estrange him even more from the family. We see that Terry is not oppressed, but instead rebels in a hostile fashion. And there is no other way he could act to counter his father's attack on the very foundation of his individuality.

A parent such as Terry's father is a negative force, since he has no essential respect for his child as a separate person. There can be no communication between parent and child while the parent refuses to recognize his child's form of suffering, his problems, and the sphere of activity in which they take place. It is natural for Terry to rebel and make certain that his reality is composed of everything his parents left out of theirs.

On the other hand, teenagers confronted by a parent such as Terry's father must try to understand what motivates this kind of parent to act as he does. Terry's father worked his way up in the world, and his success makes him believe that his formula is the best one for attaining a position of prestige in society. His concern for his child is real, and though it may not be tempered by understanding, it can only cause more pain on all sides to call such a parent senile, and to deny his experience, which is real enough. In addition, Terry has given up on his parents and he makes no attempt to explain his needs or his point of view. Terry's mother, for instance, might never agree with him, but she could at least be helped to understand and respect his point of view. It is Terry's job to convince her that his concerns and interests are genuine, and that he knows how to live safely, even though he smokes marijuana occasionally.

The Bordens

The Bordens, unlike Dr. Henderson and her husband, present the dual aspects of the permissive parent. They base their idea of parenthood on friendship between various members of the family.

Their children are urged to express their ideas, and these are taken as valid statements. Mr. Borden talks *to* his children, not *at* them, as all too many parents are in the habit of doing. A basic feeling of trust exists in the family, and there is a good deal of communication. However, the permissive model can also present some hazards for the parent. The "buddy" aspect of the parent can be abused so that he has no control whatsoever over the children. Mr. Borden is prepared to set limits — to tell his children, for example, that he does not encourage drug-taking, that he does not agree with their judgment on the black boy. He stresses that there are non-chemical means of turning on, and is not afraid that this will lower him in his children's esteem. In our experience, this is an effective parental tactic.

Mrs. Borden — and this is an attitude prevalent amongst permissive parents — is afraid she will not be liked by her children if she opposes their views on the black boy, so she agrees with their judgment even though she has doubts about it. The parent who tries to win his children over at any expense and agrees with them almost out of fear of their disapproval, may find himself totally helpless. This totally permissive attitude is dangerous to the child who needs a sense of structure, a certain number of limits within which he can grow and against which he can rebel. Otherwise his world may become formless and threatening to him, for he has no point of view from which he can evaluate experience.

This fear of setting limits of any kind may also force the parent into a serious inconsistency, which can gravely mar his child's sense of security and the parent's own credibility. The parent who has been unwilling to set limits often finds himself reacting hysterically or in an authoritarian manner. Mrs. Borden, who is envious of her children's admiration for her husband, first tries to overwhelm Pat with affection, and then, feeling slighted, sternly rebukes her for using four-letter words — a thing which she is apparently permitted to do at home, and which Mrs. Borden, herself, indulges in. When she is baited by Pat, who has heard her refer to blacks in an insulting way, Mrs. Borden finds she has to defend herself for her indiscretion — a second inconsistency. This kind of almost casual inconsistency is seen by children — who often do not take into account the reasons behind their parents' actions — as hypocrisy. Taken to an extreme, it can lead to a serious lack of trust between young and adult members of the family.

In our experience with permissive parents, we have found that there is often a discrepancy between the values parents profess to believe in and live by, and the way they actually act in moments of familial stress. Mrs. Borden, we can assume, holds fairly liberal views on the racial situation, but should her daughter start dating a black, it is likely that she would react with anger and forbid her daughter to continue to see him. Professed liberal attitudes are often brought to the test within the home and found to be unsound. What is permissible for others can be threatening when it happens to one's own children. If parents were to envisage the possibility of children taking their attitudes at face value and acting upon them, before they profess to hold liberal views, their children's accusations of hypocrisy would be less likely and there would be more place for open discussion, rather than heated argument within the family.

Mrs. Borden's tactic of insinuating her children into the battle which is taking place between herself and her husband is also a harmful one. Treating adolescent children as friends generally has a positive effect; but using them either as confidants or tools in a struggle between husband and wife is inadvisable. Of the many adolescents we have dealt with, none have wished to know of the marital difficulties their parents may be having. All of them have expressed resentment and contempt toward their parents for attempting to involve them in this manner. Marital difficulties openly threaten the security of the family, and hence, of the child. Furthermore, adolescents tend to be very puritanical when it comes to their parents' relationships. The attempt to gain the affection of a child at the expense of the other parent generally results in the child's turning to the other parent, or rejecting both of them. Thus, the details of parental strife and problems should not be shared. However, it is equally important to realize that the existence of marital strife usually *cannot* be hidden, and thus that total denial should not be attempted. Hence, parents can acknowledge the fact that they are having difficulties, but avoid turning their adolescents into confidants.

The insecurity which Mrs. Borden experiences with her children is typical of many modern parents. She *demands* love from them and constant reaffirmation of their approval of her. Children, sensing this weakness and helplessness, often turn on such a parent, as Pat did in this case. Children need to believe that parents are strong creatures who can guide them into adult life, and will not easily forgive their helplessness. This is not to say that every parent must become a bulwark of security overnight. However, it is helpful for a parent to realize that often *demands* for love, for respect, etc., may be unrealistic and unwarranted.

Because her insecurity makes Mrs. Borden overly sensitive to her children's attitudes toward her, she tends to over-react when she feels insulted or hurt. This prevents her from being able to handle family situations. She must learn that children do not always hurt a parent intentionally, nor do they always mean what they say — though they mean it for that moment. The parent should maintain a sufficient distance from a situation involving adolescents to be able to judge what stance it is best to take next, so that there is no harsh over-reaction nor unnecessary tension.

Teenagers as mature as the elder Borden children seem to be should, however, try to act sensitively toward their parents and not needle the point of tension. Parents, after all, are people with real feelings, who cannot always be totally consistent in their actions. Pat's attitude toward her mother, though it is a typical one, is unduly harsh and makes her mother's burden of nervousness even harder to bear.

Mrs. Rojack

Mrs. Rojack is an example of the detached parent. Seen from the outside, this kind of parent can appear ideal, but in reality, this is the kind of parent that can be most harmful to a child's development. Anthony is given complete freedom. There are no arguments in the house. Furthermore, Mrs. Rojack presents him with innumerable material advantages, and it is significant that the only instance in our profile when she seeks him out, rather than vice versa, is when she wishes to give him his allowance. But the lack of warmth, of emotional involvement and contact, can drive a child to extremities in order to obtain some kind of reaction from his parent. Emotional interaction is lacking in the Rojack household. Mrs. Rojack salves her conscience, her intimation that she is perhaps not doing full justice to her motherhood, by giving Anthony things. This combination of material benefits and emotional uninvolvement is deceptive, and the parent should never allow himself to believe that he has provided for his child's welfare merely because he has endowed him with material advantages.

Mrs. Rojack, just like her husband, is caught up in her own work. One would suppose that a social worker, who deals with children continuously, would be able to handle her son in an appropriate manner. Unfortunately, it is often the case that such people expect their own home situations to take care of themselves. Anthony is left to his own devices, and feeling abandoned, attempts to evoke a response from his mother by acting ill. The problem here is not whether he is actually ill or not, but that his acting out of illness is a distinct appeal for contact, for love. The young crave security, affection, and acceptance and will go to great lengths to attain this from their parents or peers. However, if positive reaffirmation is lacking from their parents, they prefer an emotional voicing of disapproval to a total lack of reaction. At least, the child reasons, the parent's anger means he *cares*.

Mrs. Rojack responds to Anthony's overt plea for attention in an all-too-casual manner. She tells him that she has more important things on her mind. This may be true here, but one has the feeling that this scene has taken place time and again, with Anthony's pleas becoming more and more extravagant, while Mrs. Rojack constantly avoids any kind of direct confrontation. If this kind of family interaction, or rather, lack of interaction, goes on, it is very possible that Anthony will take an overdose, as he threatens to do, merely to obtain some undivided attention. It is also likely that this absence of emotion in the family relationship will result in a deadening of his emotions, and hence, lead to a search for greater and greater stimulation on his part, as well as an inability to relate to people outside the family.

When Anthony mentions that he is feeling ill because he has taken some pills, Mrs. Rojack is afraid to get too involved in the situation by asking him what kind, or how many. She reassures herself by remembering that she has given Anthony a book on drugs. By reacting in this way, Mrs. Rojack is shirking her responsibility as a parent, a too-frequent phenomenon in the contemporary family. It is up to her, if she wishes to try to prevent heavy drug use on Anthony's part, to confront him on this issue. But she chooses not to do so. Her whole attitude is one of harried disaffection mingled with an unwillingness to accept Anthony's suffering — and the physical here is only a metaphor for the psychic — as real.

Once Anthony has been rejected by his mother in his plea for affection, he naturally turns on her. He attacks her where he thinks it will hurt her most — her pride in her work, her life's activity. This hostile tactic of negating the validity of a whole sphere of activity is a common one amongst rebellious teenagers. Mrs. Rojack begins by reacting to it appropriately, in that she does not blow up and scream at Anthony. The positive thing to do here, if a dialogue between parent and child is to evolve, is to recognize the views of the teenager and then say, "But I *do* know a little more about this than you," and then proceed to show how whatever is in question is in some way a valid or necessary activity. Mrs. Rojack's calm, however, is only a screen against any possible further involvement with Anthony. She is threatened by his criticism and his overt hostility, and does not know how to turn the situation into a fruitful exchange between mother and child. She simply orders Anthony from the room and tells him to listen to his latest material acquisition.

Anthony's hostility is once again a hidden demand for affection. When this is not forthcoming, he confronts his mother with a feat which he is sure will draw her complete attention, together with an examination of his problems. He claims that he has been playing truant. Again, Mrs. Rojack refuses to believe that there is any real problem here, only a childish whim, an impertinence committed by a grown youth. She offers to send Anthony away, give him a change of scene. This, in a sense, precisely sums up her whole attitude to Anthony: a refusal to recognize the reality of his suffering together with an attempt to avoid problems and any direct confrontation. Anthony correctly interprets this, though perhaps in a slightly exaggerated manner — as a desire to be rid of him totally, and he feels that his mother might as well ship him off to his death.

Mr. Rojack, like his wife, has neither the time nor the desire to examine what may be wrong with his son. There is no easy solution to this kind of family dilemma, except perhaps to warn parents like the Rojacks that their detachment may drive their children to seriously destructive acts. The adolescent who senses that his parents are too threatened by his presence to react to it, and who feels that they are avoiding his real difficulties, should however, think twice before allowing himself to get caught up in a stream of activity aimed at shocking his parents into emotion. A constant search for extravagant acts can result in a deadening of one's own emotions, and might very well ruin one's future possibilities.

used too often

Being a parent, especially of an adolescent youngster, can be a difficult task. Based on our experience, we have suggested that there are ways of handling tense situations which are likely to have positive results, and ways which are likely to have negative results. Both adults and teenagers crave affection, approval, and reaffirmation, and it is especially important that within the family a sense of security based on these should exist.

CULTURE AND
COUNTER CULTURE

THE GENERATION
GAP

Possibly the simplest method of approaching the major social, political, and psychological issues which separate the generations is to describe the values of old and young in juxtaposition. It will then be clear how in some cases the values of the young embody a direct reaction against the older generation while in other cases the values of the young are the articulated expression of what was already inherent, and either repressed or unexpressed, in the older generation. This is not to say that every individual lives according to a clearly defined ethic, or that every teenager could articulate that against which he is rebelling, or with which he is discontented. However, our actions, our life styles, do represent what is perhaps an unconscious ethic. Ideology, at its simplest and yet most profound level, is precisely what our actions betray in our day-to-day lives: *what and how we live.*

There is one item which must be mentioned at the beginning of any discussion of the youth culture, though it is often omitted: not all adolescents are ardent radicals, hippies, yippies, street people, or dropouts — the sectors of the adolescent population that the media, with its eye for color, has chosen to publicize. The more reactionary groups, always on the lookout for an issue that will channel attention away from more pressing problems, have, regrettably, reinforced this view.

interesting

85

Radicals do exist, as the most articulate sector of the youth culture; they act as catalysts for feelings and half-formed ideas which lie dormant in the minds of many less extreme youngsters, who may not totally approve of the actions of their more radical peers.

The Protestant Ethic

At the core of the American cultural experience lies the "Protestant Ethic," which stresses the value of work over pleasure and immediate gratification. Work is the emblem of the good life, the test of individual character; it constitutes the central phase of an existence directed toward a distant future where the rewards of work will be harvested. Linked to the primary importance of work in the Protestant Ethic is the power of each individual man to change, better, or control his existence and environment, to play a significant part in human *progress*. The Protestant Ethic has shaped the actions and reactions, in their widest contours, of generations of Americans. Within our own time, one can safely speculate that most parents have lived according to the Protestant Ethic, and most of today's young people are reacting against it.

Most parents of today's adolescents lived out their childhoods during the days of the depression. Their earliest memories reach back to this difficult period, and its formative influence on their lives cannot be underestimated. When the very substances for life are lacking — food, shelter, clothing — then it is only natural that these obviously material needs be stressed. It obviously follows that the sanctity of work was encouraged and emphasized by the particular set of social conditions which governed most parents' early lives. Thus, one finds the roots of the current parental generation's preoccupation with material success in the depression.

The emphasis on living standards which came out of the depression was based upon the notion that fulfillment will somehow be found once a sufficient number of material goods have been secured. The ceiling on acquisition, however, is almost never reached. The consumer society is in full swing these days: happiness is just another car or color television set away. And somewhere along the road to a constant increase in the standard of living, the value of life itself is lost.

The belief that further material acquisitions can cure human discontent is accompanied in the parental generation by the empha-

86

sis placed on work. It is through work that one attains "success" — a higher standard of living, a greater annual income. One works today to reap tomorrow, and meanwhile today is obliterated. The distant plateau of a future when all those desires repressed or submerged during the work days can finally be played out in a golden twilight of leisure is, however, so rarely reached. The story of the successful businessman who dies on the eve of his retirement is tragically common in this decade of American history. Those who do live long enough to retire have often lost the very capacity for enjoyment. The working habit has become so great that it has killed man's ability to immerse himself wholly in any other kind of activity.

This is a critical view of the parental generation's emphasis on material acquisition — a view frequently stressed by the young. But the spirit of this criticism is not the sole property, or even the invention, of today's counter culture. It is something which the parents of today's adolescents themselves have, perhaps unconsciously, transmitted to them, in one way or another. During a short phase in its own youth, the parental generation itself levelled a form of criticism against the American ethic of success. The young of the early 1950's talked disparagingly of "keeping up with the Joneses." In *The Man in the Gray Flannel Suit,* a popular novel and film, they found the crystalization of their intuition that the life of the so-called "organization man" was one of banality and futility. The widely read *What Makes Sammy Run* pointed out the ruthlessly dehumanizing aspects of the business world. Aware of the faults of the working world into which they were about to enter, the parental generation still had little choice but to quell its misgivings and participate in this very world. Generally, however, they communicated their now somewhat submerged misgivings and dissatisfaction to their children. The father who comes home from work feeling irritated and harassed to growl at his wife and children, or simply to retreat to television and bed, is overtly manifesting his dissatisfaction or discouragement with the world where material prosperity is the symbol of fulfillment.

Shaped in this atmosphere of dissatisfaction, today's adolescents have merely articulated a criticism of the materialistic ethic which has been latently present among many of their parents. Once voiced, this criticism is often so threatening to parents that it makes them react harshly — precisely because they sense its validity and recognize the fact that they are no longer able to change their own lives.

In other words, those criticisms which bear some element of truth are those which hurt most deeply. A dialogue between the generations can be created only when the young realize that their parents, too, have lived through a phase of criticism of the materialist-success ethic, and only when parents are willing to admit that they are not fully satisfied with the life-course which existing conditions have forced them to take.

If the two cultures we are speaking of are to reach any form of understanding, we must look a little deeper into the emotional and intellectual underpinnings of the forty-to-fifty-year-olds' insistence on material welfare, and the implications this background has with regard to such issues as war. Two world-shaking events impinged upon the parental generation's consciousness. One, as noted before, was the depression; the second was the Second World War. Even if the individual himself was not directly involved in these events, they pervaded the atmosphere of his formative years and helped to shape his world view. The depression, as we have already mentioned, threatened the material well-being of the entire country. Economic bankruptcy created a nationwide feeling of frightening defeat, and this common experience instilled in the American people a solidarity on one issue: confrontation with the government that had been discredited in their eyes must ensue. This distrust of the government's ability to provide for and manage the country was similar to the credibility gap that exists today between young people and their parents as well as their government.

However, the war which followed on the heels of the depression brought America to victory on international fronts and seemed to wipe out material threat. Fighting against tyranny in Europe and against aggressors in the East, America rose from its feeling of defeat. The war not only brought victory, but marked the end of depression, the beginning of a new period of prosperity, and trust in the governmental powers which had forged all this. In the eyes of the parental generation, formed by this experience, war can be a just act, directed against tyrannies, fought in the name of democracy. War is somehow associated in their minds with a return to material stability. Little wonder then, that this attitude persisted uncritically into the period of the cold war and lingers on in many Americans of the older generation today. The country's victory in the Second World War is at the heart of current American optimism: the trust that all will turn out well in the end. For if a country can survive

88

the depression and emerge victorious from it, surely it must be able to survive almost anything.

This capsule and greatly oversimplified social history helps us to understand why the parental culture and the adolescent culture have such difficulty understanding each other. The young, because of their particular experience, find it hard to understand and believe that the lives of their parents have ever been materially threatened, that they have experienced defeat and hence have a cogent reason for stressing material welfare (and, for that matter, professional education, which tends to see one through most periods of financial crisis). Furthermore, young people cannot see that war, from the parents' historical viewpoint, is not an immoral act, but necessary in the struggle against tyranny — whatever mistaken countries the powers-that-be may cite as potentially tyrannical and threatening. On the other hand, parents often refuse to admit, from the vantage point of their own material experience, that anyone who has everything — as their affluent children do — can possibly feel defeated or unfulfilled (even though, as we have mentioned, many of them went through a brief period in which they, themselves, were critical of the materialist ethic).

Unlike their parents, the bulk of American youth, whether they be upper, middle, or working class, were born and raised in a society of relative affluence. Material possessions have always been at their disposal, along with the manifold possibilities created by affluence: higher education and a choice of careers. Consequently, the work ethic and the emphasis on a constantly higher standard of living appears to them as a sterile negation of life. They feel their parents are achieving nothing but an exaltation of their own ego in their long working hours, the barren ritual of climbing the ladder of success. The teenager recognizes that in his parents' material preoccupations, whole aspects of life have been forgotten. He rebels against this view of life and tries to live out in his own life everything that his parents have left out of theirs.

Thus we see in the children of so-called "uptight" parents an attempt to re-introduce joy and sensual gratification into life, an attempt to greet the whole impulse-life of man. Children of urban dwellers suddenly recognize the beauty of the country, the marvels of natural life. They delight in a free and open sexuality; they idealize spontaneity of feeling and reject the parental insistence on repression of impulse so that long-term goals can be obtained.

While their parents have always looked to the future as a vague, unspecified period when their aims will have been attained — when they will be free to relax and fulfill their deepest dreams — contemporary young people are oriented toward the present. In all senses of the word, they are the NOW generation. When the spectre of total atomic annihilation haunts the world, futurity becomes a meaningless concept. Tomorrow may never come. Hence everything that must be done, or experienced, must occur today. Whether it be a trip to California, which means dropping out of school, or a need to rectify the inequities of our social system, immediacy is the younger generation's keyword. The possibility of a radical end, it seems, necessitates a radical life style. This is why so many of the more intelligent teenagers today lean toward radical politics, toward activism of various kinds. The grindings of the congressional machine function at all too leisurely a pace to solve pressing problems while they can still be solved.

What the parental generation often fails to understand is that it is precisely the security, the material affluence, of young people's experience today that gives them the leisure and necessary distance to be able to criticize the military attitude linked to optimism which is their parents'. Their short past has shown them that it is precisely war abroad that helps the country to maintain its affluence. While arms and all their related goods are being produced, the wheels of industry turn.

But wars, from the standpoint of today's adolescents, are never just wars. Hiroshima, to them, is not a just retaliation for Pearl Harbor, but an immoral assault that devastated the lives of an entire generation. The war in Vietnam is not an attempt to put down a threatening totalitarian state, nor an effort to maintain so-called "world peace," but a useless destruction of lives. While their parents are still caught up in the attitude that all wars are a prolongation of the victorious and necessary effort of the Second World War, young people feel that a new era has been entered upon in which this "world view" cannot hold. Varying material experiences necessarily imply varying ideologies. Perhaps it is only when the veterans of Vietnam — and this is the NOW generation's war despite themselves — can confront their parents with their own war experience, that some kind of understanding can be reached between the two opposed poles. The fact that ever larger sectors of the American population are turning against the war in Vietnam is due, at least in part, to

the fact that young Vietnam veterans are themselves voicing disapproval of the war. Pragmatic experience, in American culture,
has always been the ultimate test of the validity of an attitude.

Enmeshed in the whirlpool of consumerism, work, and the desire
for higher profits, the parental generation had little time to spare
to cast a glance at the fate of their fellow men or their environment.
While portions of the population prospered, ghettos burgeoned in
the center of the metropolis: a cancerous growth in the midst of
the American dream. Columns of steel, concrete, and glass thrust
their way higher and deeper into the atmosphere, dwarfing man
or entombing him. In search of profits, but under the guise of cold
war politics, neighboring and distant countries suffered American
policemen, American investment, American exploitation. At home,
still in the search for profits and increasingly greater expediency,
the environment was depleted, our rivers, our forests, and the very
air polluted. Or so it seemed to the child of affluence who suddenly
awoke in adolescence and took a look around him.

Since we are speaking of general trends here, rather than isolated
individuals, one can safely say that the lives of the parental generation gave them little time or inclination to concern themselves with
larger social problems. The population explosion, pollution, racism,
poverty, all, until very recently, went relatively unnoticed by the
greater part of the country. Non-human elements, material goods,
had taken precedence over human life and human values. Man had
become alienated from man, open to use as an object rather than
as a living being. However, the dawning adolescent was struck by the
material security of, let us say, his own suburban home and the
poverty of the city nearby. He noticed the contradiction between
his own sheltered affluence and the plight of some of his school-
mates; his parents' uncritical acceptance of the status quo. Having
been reared by fairly permissive parents who encouraged self-
expression in their young if not in themselves, having been educated
in schools which spoke of such things without perhaps fully connecting them to the system, the youngster gave vent to his feelings.
And a social conscience was infused into the mainstream of affluent
life.

Contemporary youth have, if anything, a highly moral approach
to life. It is a morality which is not often attached to any traditional
political vision; nor does it have to protect itself against any entrenched interests, since the young do not feel materially threatened

by the possibility of another kind of life. Rather, this morality is based on a strongly personal sense of justice, on an ability to cut through hypocrisies and lies to the core of a problem, and on a wish to dignify man. It is a reaction against what the young see as their parents' personal irresponsibility vis-à-vis their fellow man, and against the organized irresponsibility of the establishment which dehumanizes life — something they have all personally experienced in the nation's public schools. This politics of morality finds its vent in whatever issue happens to come up in a given area: the Free Speech Movement at Berkeley, protest against racist behavior by a local teacher or landlord, demonstrations against the war in Vietnam, or, within the home, the hypocrisy of a parent.

Against what they see as the aridity of their parents' lives, the robot-like precision with which they carry out their daily affairs, the young set up the value of personal or spiritual development. They believe that fulfillment will not come from the further acquisition of material goods — a trend which they sense only entrenches the already prevalent treatment of man as an object to be used, profited by, and then thrust aside. Thus, they value inner space, personalism, and they seek to create, almost simplistically, relationships based on love. Since the established religions have become associated with the sterility of the "system," they turn increasingly to oriental cults which stress self-development rather than organized doctrine. Or they look to magic, nature cults, and drugs in an effort to reinstill a religious awe, a spirituality into mechanized life.

Technology, Technocracy, and the Reverence of Expertise

American society has a deeply entrenched, optimistic belief in the power of the machine. Through technological advances, the creed goes, man will increasingly be freed from the burdens of existence and provided with the leisure in which to make truly human and creative use of his life. This is the traditional justification for technological progress. But there are grave dangers inherent in technological progress which are only beginning to be widely understood. The young, born into the midst of a computer age, are the first, as a group, to manifest overtly their dissatisfaction with technology and technocracy — that system of bureaucrats and experts which virtually runs this society. The advent of electronic communication and rapid transportation has made it increasingly

92

possible for a relatively small number of men to control and co-ordinate their fellows. The young may not be the first to articulate a critique of this system, nor are many of them capable of expressing their dissatisfaction in theoretical terms, but their actions, their rebelliousness, and the life styles they admire, all reveal that the cult of technology has been discredited in their eyes. When affluence exists, together with the technological means for eradicating such problems as pollution, poverty, and over-population, it is totally disheartening to see that these means are not being utilized for the improvement of man's human condition. If parents are to understand their children's dissatisfaction, their feeling of defeat in the midst of affluence, it is necessary for them to examine their own feelings and to glance at the wider implications of our technological world.

We are all, thanks to the media, now familiar with the more obvious dangers of a technological progress unchecked by human or moral values. The growing efficiency of super-weapons which could bring a cataclysmic end to the world has made us all stop and take note. So, too, has the threat of total depletion, the poisoning of our environment caused by the unlimited expansion of industry, weapon-testing, and over-production of such seemingly essential consumer items as cars. And we now have not quite so much faith in the power of technology to solve the ills we have allowed it to produce. However, these are only the more immediately visible dangers of technological progress. It is the subtle, more insidious effects of technology which the young are sensitive to and which must be recognized and articulated by both generations.

The first of these is our society's tendency to value what is most machine-like, most computer-like in man, since this, it is believed, will ensure the efficient and rational functioning of our world. Thus, objectivity is valued, trusted, because the person who is capable of standing apart from himself, his own feelings, and his prejudices will, it is felt, be able to give us a just evaluation of any problem or fact. The growth of such "human" sciences as sociology, which attempt to throw an impersonal, statistical light on human life, runs parallel to the enshrinement of objectivity.

Secondly, there is our reverence of expertise. The experts, those gentlemen who claim to hold the keys to technological reality and to have exhausted all knowledge in one particular field, have been granted god-like authority. We have given complete freedom to scientists, military tacticians, experts in foreign affairs, educators, doctors, managers, and technicians to function as they please without the threat or check of outside criticism. In other words, the people have abandoned all control of the powers that actually govern their lives, their destiny, and their children's destiny. The geneticist is free to experiment with the development of test-tube life with little popular thought to the vast repercussions this could have. Naval engineers and military researchers can collaborate on ways of creating weather control which could alter the agricultural possibilities of an enemy country. Military tacticians and foreign affairs experts tell us, only after the event, that they have found it strategic to infiltrate a distant country.

The experts' realm of knowledge apparently cannot even be communicated in the language of mere mortal men; they shroud their work in jargon — "correlations," "parameters," "non-normative optimizations," and "mathematical formulas" — only comprehensible to themselves. The regime of experts therefore functions free of criticism, free of any outside checks, since we have immunized it in an untouchable sphere of incomprehensibility.

What this deification of objectivity and expertise means in non-technological and human terms, however, is something quite different. The value we have placed on orderliness, the ability to face routine, on self-control, and on specialization — all qualities, incidentally, that our school system attempts to instill in the young — merely serve, at best, to produce a well-programmed machine, not a fully alive human being. Objectivity may be a positive scientific asset, but transposed to a human sphere it actually means alienation. The man who is capable of producing a space in himself where he is not himself, but a well-ordered and rational computer, is estranged from himself: his feelings, the demands of his body, and if you will, his psyche. He cannot immerse himself in a natural environment, nor relate wholly to a fellow being, for his most familiar self is only attuned to analysis, self-control, the negation of feeling. He is depersonalized, dehumanized.

Brought up on the American political philosophy, which speaks of democracy and the sanctity and power of the individual to govern his destiny, his ability to participate in the management of his country, it is no wonder that young people today are disillusioned by the state of their society. The government has discredited itself, as far as they are concerned, and they refuse to trust the abstract

94

workings of the all-powerful "system." They recognize that the society in which they have been raised has exalted objectivity at the cost of humanity, and expertise at the cost of idealism and imagination. They rebel against the so-called realistic and practical outlook which envisages only short-range aims and empirical goals. They drop out of school because the educational institutions train them only to adapt to this dehumanizing system and succeed as another alienated expert or technocrat. What they desire instead is a system of ethics, a human morality that could be reinstilled into technocracy, so that man once again could *master* the machine, rather than build himself in its image.

The "objective" language which technocracy has created for itself is a language of conscious obfuscation and mystification which only serves to negate the human reality or the human implications of any given situation. Life and death are forgotten in abstractions. Thus, the reckoning of the numbers of dead in the battlefields of Vietnam becomes a "body count." The "struggle for peace" is a euphemism for outright war. A "strategic hamlet" is a concentration camp. The "kill ratio" stands for a comparison of the slaughter of the two sides engaged in battle. To drop more bombs on a small Asian country than were dropped in Europe during the entire Second World War is "escalation." The list is endless, but all the terms imply that not a drop of human blood has stained the clean white gloves of our military experts.

The logistics sphere is not the only one where language has lost its relation to the actuality of human life. We have all glanced at medical, psychiatric, sociological, scientific and technical journals, only to find them totally incomprehensible. It is not that what they are trying to express is always so inordinately difficult, merely that a supposedly objective "scientized" jargon has taken over. The search for a depersonalized rationality has over-stepped itself and succeeded in creating a new kind of religion: a cult of expertise whose hieroglyphics are comprehensible only to the initiate.

It is no wonder then that a credibility gap exists between young and old, between youth and the establishment. The terminology of the experts is meaningless to the young: a series of illusions or lies. They see through such neutral terms as "body count" to the bloody reality beneath. After all, the bodies being counted are those of their friends. When even words ripe with historical implications, such as "democracy," "liberty," and "equality," have lost any

95

relationship to the reality at hand, little credibility can remain in words. Thus we have the phenomenon of youth's insistence on using the simplest and often the crudest of terms — those which still have some emotional impact and carry a vital human charge. We begin to understand why the young so often insist that words are only the very topmost surface of human communication. In reaction to the scientized jargon of the technocrats, the young have created their own language of feeling and sensation: of being "high" or "stoned," of "diggers" and being "hip," of suggestive "Ya, man's" and exclamations.

It is perhaps necessary to mention here that there is as great a danger in the young's distrust of language as in their elder's objective jargon. Both are reductionist and stress only one aspect of man's possibilities. Words are, after all, one of the distinguishing features of man and still our most common form of communication. To reduce language to its barest essentials will not result in a greater humanization, but merely another distortion of the total being. If the intellect — the reasoning power of man — is neglected in favor of feeling, or a worship of the irrational, then we are confronted with a different kind of estrangement — one which is potentially as destructive to life as our present alienation. Both sides of the dichotomy, young and old, must be integrated if youth's ideal of transforming the very "sense men have of reality" is to be achieved.

At the Other End of the Spectrum: Participational Democracy

The young have formed their world outlook in reaction to the technocratic manipulation of their lives. They are fascinated by magic, ritual, tribal lore, and the psychedelic experience — the whole spectrum of human possibility which lies at the opposite pole from managerial self-control and the objective rational consciousness. Thus a march on Washington may entail a magical attempt to exorcise the White House. Folk rock is based on thumping primitive rhythms. Tarot cards, horoscopes, books on magic, abound in the stores the young frequent.

At the root of the participational democracy that many young people desire as an antidote to the technocratic democracy that has made a mockery of the individual's part in the functioning of the nation lies a nostalgia for the primitive tribe or village in which

96

each individual plays a telling part in the structure of the whole. The youth communes across the country are in some ways the incarnation of the young's ideal of participational democracy. They are an attempt to set up an alternate culture based precisely on the values which the older generation has obliterated in itself. Unlike radical youth, most commune dwellers are not directly confronting the system; but both groups believe that there must be a re-evaluation of man's life, a learning to live in a different way according to different values, before our society can reflect man in all his human dignity.

Adults who contend that the radical young are being simplistic or naive in their desire to create a participational democracy and a new life style are failing to see the importance of the counter culture. While participational democracy may well be unfeasible in our highly complex civilization, the critique of the present system that the young embody in their desires, their values, their music, and their clothes should not be underrated. They *are* correct in their emphasis on the fact that our technological society has engendered a depersonalization of man so great that individual life has been rendered almost valueless.

On the other hand, the young who demand immediate change from their parents and accuse them of hypocrisy when they speak of American democracy must try to understand that it is virtually impossible for an adult, faced by the responsibility of supporting a family, to leave the organization he works for because it supports the system in some way. Nor is it always possible for a parent to alter radically a life pattern which has existed for years. A dialogue between the generations can only occur once both sides have taken the other's point of view into consideration.

If we continue speaking of cultural trends here, rather than of historical or current particulars, then we must isolate one more generalized characteristic that distinguishes the adult culture from the counter culture. American society has traditionally focused its dreams and aspirations on the winner: that hardy, usually aggressive, figure who can triumph over nature, like the pioneer or the astronaut, who can excel over his peers like the prosperous business-man of myth who started as a shoemaker and ended as a wealthy magnate, or the lowly private, who can come home from the wars a beribboned master sergeant, a hero. These are only a few examples, but they reveal the pressure that conventional society exerts on man to rise above his own position, intellectually, financially, or physically. America is the inheritor and last resting place of the myth of Faustian man, metaphorically going out to conquer new worlds.

Psychologically, this is a "masculine" orientation. The human qualities America values are those linked with extroversion: going out of oneself to succeed in some field of endeavor. Rationality and personal objectivity in any given situation — as we have mentioned in our discussion of the technological, objective man — are stressed. Fulfillment is placed somewhere outside the self, either in a profession, or in the attainment of material things, and it is labelled "success." This emphasis on rationality presupposes an emphasis on order and all its social equivalents: the policeman, the judge, the state. On the individual level, it suggests that spontaneity, instinct, emotions, and sensibility should be suppressed in favor of organized action and self-control.

As in other spheres, here too, the young embody precisely what their parents have suppressed or considered negative. The youth culture is largely feminine in orientation, and this does not mean that it is effeminate or homosexual. The man of action is rejected in favor of the introspective, sensitive individual who finds his fulfillment in inwardness and in human relationships. "Make love, not war;" "flower-power," not arms; is the hippie ethic, and though in this era of quick turnover in fashion hippiedom is more or less dead, the values the hippies sloganized are still very much part of the youth culture. Even among the young political radicals who would seem to fall more closely within the range of the "masculine" image, there is a tendency to value inwardness and personalism, though these are the ends, not the means of revolution. Rationality and self-control are rejected. Taking their place are spontaneity, magic, and, often, an amorphous spirituality. The so-called feminization of the young American male — his long hair, his interest in music rather than sports, his unaggressive stance — are all symptomatic of this new orientation.

So, too, is the young's choice of drugs as the symbol of their generation. Marijuana and the psychedelics are drugs which turn one inward to one's unconscious mind. The young believe these drugs make them more sensitive to music, to nature, to painting, and to each other, expanding consciousness beyond the rational limit. Whether the values accorded to these drugs by the young have a factual basis is something we discuss in the next chapter.

The "Loser" vs. the "Winner"

In place of the traditional American focus on the winner, today's young people model themselves on the "loser." They have turned the conventional ethic upside down. In some cases this is truly a gesture of solidarity, but most often solidarity is only the superficial excuse. The roots of this identification lie deeper, as we shall see in a moment. Beads and buckskins relate the young to the Indians, the victims of American genocide. So too does their use of such drugs as peyote, the primitive rhythms of their music, and the aspect of a tribal function which so many rock-festivals take on. From the blacks, or rather the American myth of the blacks — for it would be outright disparagement to call this a total reality — the young have taken their "hang-loose" ethic: the insistence on keeping cool, on open sexuality, and on frenetic rhythms. They have elevated dirt and the dole — the ironical privilege of the poor man — to a mystique. To go the way of ghetto youth has become an ideal filled with thrills and the possibility of perversity. Pushers and hustlers form a young elite because they dare to defy the law, the regime of order.

This deification and emulation of the "loser" (and we must remember here that we are not speaking about all youth, but of cultural trends) is, as we have suggested, rarely a true gesture of solidarity with the oppressed. For affluent youth to model themselves on these topsy-turvy values is to perpetrate a form of slander against the oppressed. The poor and the blacks live as they do out of necessity, not out of a search for thrills or cheap sensation. True revolutionaries tend to be puritanical, as Mao's China and Castro's Cuba reveal. The youth who feels he must follow his peers in their idealization of the loser should perhaps question his motives before embarking on a path which is only glamorous on the glossy pages of Life magazine.

Why then has this deification of the loser taken place? The media, who seek out sensationalism in all its forms, have of course something to do with glamorizing the life of the street people or hippies. But the roots of the problem probably lie deeper, in the inordinate pressures American society focuses on the individual. Success, in whatever field, is imperative, or so the myth of the winner tells us. Otherwise, one is lost in nonentity, in oblivion. The child, confronted with this burden of success, this onus of extraordinariness, finds as he grows up that it is exceedingly difficult to become a winner in this highly complex, modern world. One's ambition must be almost superhuman, and so narrowly focused as to block out all other interests and possibilities, whether they be relationships or achievements.

Competition, even to enter a good university, is fierce. And often, if ambition is present, native talent and aptitude do not match it. But to resign oneself to mediocrity, to be merely "good" after one has been raised with excessive expectations — and American parents frequently demand the impossible from their children — is not so easy. It is, or so it seems to youth, to resign oneself to oblivion.

The Real Dilemma: How to Be Special?

What, then? The simplest answer is to become extraordinary in some less demanding way: to turn to negative extremes such as excessive drug-taking, dropping out of school, pushing, or various non-conventional forms of sexuality. This ensures the possibility of attention without undue demands on perseverance, intellect, or native talent. The danger of this negative ethic to the individual and the society around him cannot be underestimated.

Recognition from one's peers or superiors has long been of primary importance in the American way of life, and it is not surprising that the young have sought this in whatever way they find possible. But it must be understood, by parents and young people alike, that recognition in this increasingly pluralistic world of ours is not the only measure of individual worth. To be outstanding does not necessarily mean that one is in any way a better, more dignified, or more human person. It is people as a *whole* who constitute the value of a civilization, not merely its most recognized experts or its media-created "stars."

Parents and educators themselves may be largely responsible for this last facet of the counter culture. Every individual in our society wishes to feel "special," extraordinary in some way. Such is the temper of American life. But so many parents are largely absent from the home, so many have lost contact with their children, that they have simply not been able to give their children sufficient attention to satisfy this craving to be outstanding. Similarly, schools and universities have become anonymous, depersonalized institutions, where it is almost impossible for more than a handful of

100

individuals to be recognized and attended to in the way they desire. Furthermore, parents who pressure their children to succeed at all costs, yet never express their satisfaction with what has been achieved, force their children to attempt more and more extravagant methods to gain attention. Mediocrity is, after all, only a self-evaluation, and the child or the teenager who is made to believe in his own worth, does not need to judge himself as mediocre.

We have described the counter culture as being precisely that: an attempt by the young to build a world composed of all the values that run counter to their parents'; those values their parents have left out, by choice or by necessity, of their own culture. In place of a work ethic oriented toward future goals and the acquisition of possessions, the young have emphasized pleasure, the present, and inner fulfillment. They have turned against technology and the objective consciousness in favor of personalism, irrationality, and subjective modes of expression.

If we take a closer look, however, we find that although the young speak of the value of immediate experience, of love and the necessity for close personal relationships, they are often as incapable of these as their parents. If, sometimes in defeat, sometimes in order to escape from pressure, they turn to drugs, they are only emulating their parents' own use of alcohol or pills, which block out or normalize the stresses of the world. The problems both generations face on a human level are, in many cases, the same, even if they may seem greater to the young whose powers of resistance are not so well developed.

What the young do offer in their counter culture is a critique of the world we live in, a critique which every individual who is unthreatened by change will recognize as valid and necessary. Both generations, however, must try to understand that what each embodies on its own is not sufficient to create a total ethos, a total society, or a total man. Technology cannot be done away with, nor can we return to the simple life of the tribesman, seemingly at ease in nature and with himself. Intellect and deliberation cannot, on a mass level, be replaced by spontaneity or anarchy, unless we welcome the possibility of another Nazi Germany. However, neither can we continue to value a technocracy which depersonalizes man, enters upon despised and immoral wars without restrictions, and negates the value of life itself. The gap between the generations must be bridged not only on an individual level, but on a cultural one, if we are to create a world in which the total man can be at home with himself.

The Psychology and Sociology of Adolescence

Adolescence, for most youngsters, is a time of confusion, crisis, and physical, emotional, and intellectual upheaval. The young adolescent finds himself in a stage of transition — no longer a child permitted to play and express himself freely, to delight in passing fancies, or immerse himself in them. Instead, he is required for the first time to manifest a degree of self-control and self-regulation — to *conduct* himself like an adult without the privileges of being *treated* as one. Suddenly the sheltered child's familiar world and freely wandering imagination disintegrates, and he is confronted by the reality around him: a world of brutality, violence, lies, and enormous social problems. He is expected to contemplate his future seriously, and determine his possible role in the world.

Youth is a period of experimentation. The adolescent sees himself in a variety of roles and attempts to find one which he feels will suit him best, not only in terms of a career, but in terms of personality, sexual stance, and ideological commitment. As he gropes for a personal identity, he passes through phases of extreme self-consciousness and self-doubt. Since nothing seems settled in his personal world, he may be excessively moody, irritable, and impulsive. At one moment he acts like a mature adult; at the next he reverts to childhood, demanding to be protected, loved and spoiled. His individual identity can only be consolidated when he proves himself as a separate human being. To do this he must remove himself somewhat from the childhood sanctuary of the family, rebel against it, and test his powers — sometimes in situations involving great risk — in the outside world.

The adolescent is also confronted with a series of models for emulation, together with the major symbols and values of his culture. While he can contemplate these values and try out different roles, he is not yet required to make the various compromises inherent in daily participation in adult life. Thus he casts an untarnished eye upon the world and is quick to detect hypocrisies and falsehoods. It is here, perhaps, that the true strength of youth lies. Collectively the young provide society with an idealistic force and a critical conscience which, though it has not reached full maturity,

102

often apprehends inequities before the majority of adults, who have more at stake, are willing to admit they exist.

An extended adolescence, for the larger part of the population, is a recent historical innovation. Up until the mid-nineteenth century adolescence was a luxury granted only to the privileged few. Children developed into adults almost before they had left what we now term childhood, since social and financial pressures forced them to enter the working world and take on full responsibility for their own survival. With the rise of affluence, however, we have what has been called "the increasing foetalization of the individual" — the displacement of adult responsibilities from the young to a later and later period in individual development. It is now not uncommon to find the end of adolescence in the male at the age of thirty.

The growth of higher education for the vast majority of the American public has, of course, prolonged the period in which the individual remains free from full adult status. But higher education, and the longer period of intellectual and emotional gestation it permits, is necessary in our complex technological world, where it is increasingly difficult to master the skills necessary for proficiency in any field of endeavor. The young person of today needs a longer period of adolescence, in order to choose from the hundreds of possibilities open to him and to master one. Such is the speed of our technological development. At the same time, the post-war population explosion has created a vast number of working-age youths for whom the labor market has no room. Consequently the young are urged to continue their education for ever longer periods and remain off the labor market.

The result of this affluence-bred "extended adolescence" is disturbing. There are few meaningful and responsible roles for the teenager in our society. Instead, the young are encouraged to consume without producing. In terms of playing an active part in society, the young are kept demobilized, forced to remain young. Though they often have an adult awareness of our social problems and are sufficiently competent to act, they have no real role in shaping society. Consequently, they often suffer from a sense of uselessness and boredom, and turn for distraction to drugs or any other substance or activity which can provide thrills.

Urged, or forced, to remain young as long as possible, adolescents are generally only called upon to take active part in society in one way: to provide our warrior class. From the midst of prolonged gestation, they are thrust into the midst of war and ordered to gird themselves for slaughter. The extent of the shock this enforced discontinuity will imprint on an entire generation has yet to be measured. It is not surprising, then, that the majority of young people oppose the war in Vietnam. The period of sustained leisure in which they have had time to develop a social conscience and realistically to contemplate such issues as war has led them to recognize the absurdity or immorality of America's role in Southeast Asia. They have banded together to assume a role which society only partially grants them — that of social protesters, warriors at home. And as the culture has picked up this definition of youth as the "foe at home," they have become so increasingly, since the cultural definition of age is an important constituent in a person's self-identity.

If youth is generally described as a time of crisis and internal upheaval, then it follows that in times of rapid social change, such as we live in today, the young's confusion will be even greater. When a society itself has no stable identity, when significant political shifts take place and there is no solid structure of human values in a culture, then the period of adolescence will be difficult, indeed. Children in our prosperous society grow up with the illusion that their life will be secure and comfortable. They are often not trained to work or to think, but to enjoy, to immerse themselves in the total environment of film, where everything can be experienced second hand. Television, as teachers often complain, has trained them to expect easy information, to depend less on their own intellectual powers than those of their technological environment. Adolescence reveals to the young that they have been brought up with a mystique that has little relevance to reality. There are few ready-made roles which they can easily fit into, for in this electronic age, roles are obsolete almost as soon as they are formed. Whatever values have been passed down to them by their parents they find unacceptable, since their world, as they see it, is vastly different from their parents'.

Simultaneously, there is a great deal of pressure on the adolescent. Television, films, the increase in communications and transportation, have opened up a world of unlimited possibilities and unlimited injustice. The young are aware of many more things than their parents were at the same age. They are present — via the television set — in Biafra, in Vietnam, in Israel, in Palestinian refugee camps, at Democratic conventions, at Black Panther trials. The sum of impressions and experiences they must assimilate is far greater than in any other era in history. Children of an affluent technological age, they are the prisoners of the iniquities this age has failed to eradicate. The stress on the young in our world cannot be underestimated.

And the stress is intensified by the fact that American society has always emphasized the importance of the individual over that of the group. Individual man is regarded as being able to control his environment, rather than as being subject to it. Furthermore, change and progress have always been looked upon as positive — at least as words. And the young have generally been glorified as the potential bearers of this continuous innovation. The pressure on the adolescent then, is two-fold. Not only has the cultural climate led him to believe that he will have the power to shape his personal destiny, but it has further suggested to him that he has a positive role to fulfill in bettering his society. One can imagine the adolescent's plight and confusion when, filled with this belief in his power, he is suddenly confronted by the full complexity of the adult world and the enormity of the tasks which he feels must be performed.

Very soon in his development toward adulthood he is faced by the realization that in actual fact the individual is relatively powerless — that it is almost impossible for the single person to change the face of his environment or even leave a small mark on it. His role has not been chosen for him or even suggested, since our unstructured society gives the young only amorphous hopes, not a definition of future roles, as did cultures where roles were passed down from father to son. And he is not only confronted by confusion regarding his identity, but by a sense of powerlessness aggravated by a burden of cultural pressures and hopes. One begins to understand why our affluent society is filled with so many disillusioned, despondent, and alienated adolescents.

It also then seems more logical that so many of our more articulate young are radicals who turn toward ideologies foreign to America. Lenin's Russia, Mao's China, Castro's Cuba provide them with examples of how change can be achieved. The importance here lies not in the slogans the young use — often without realizing their full implications — but in the fact that these foreign ideologies focus on the power of the group, the united force of people banded together. The individual with his limited powers is superseded by the aggregate power of the group. If another radical sector of our young speak of participational democracy, it is incomprehensible how they can be looked upon as the "enemy within." Granted that they are activists, but what they are fighting for is precisely what American culture has taught them to regard as sacred without giving them the possibility of experiencing it: the power of the individual to have a hand in controlling and changing his society and environment.

By placing it in relief, we have perhaps somewhat exaggerated the difficulty of adolescence. Not every youngster is, of course, aware of the problems we have discussed, nor does he necessarily suffer them acutely, especially in the earlier phases of adolescence when personal matters of identity and relationships with others are more central to his existence. However, if we are to understand the phenomenon of adolescence as a whole, we must take these larger social factors into consideration. There are no simple solutions to the problems we have spoken of, for they implicate our entire ethos. But should we wish to mobilize the enormous potential of extended youth, we must create responsible roles within our society which the young can take on. As things now stand, the young have an adult conscience, adult possibilities, but no adult status and rewards.

There is, however, a place in society for the youngster that is more satisfactory than the one he now holds. Youth's part in the desegregation of the South revealed their strong organizational potential, their almost unlimited energy, and their willingness to perform trivial or routine tasks when their efforts are being directed at a goal they consider worthwhile. With all the problems which exist in our contemporary world, it is absurd to allow this fund of youthful potential to go untapped. The young are certainly responsible enough to work in organizing ghetto schools or recreational activities such as street theatres or summer communes for the young or aged; in supplying aid to drug abusers and addicts; and as apprentices to various legal, medical, and social organizations.

The possibilities are limitless. All that is lacking is the willingness of the adult community to trust in their own offspring; to show the young that they, too, are concerned with the problems of the world around them as well as individual success. While there are such important social tasks to perform and such a fund of untapped energy exists in the youthful population, it is discouraging to see the adolescent wasting himself on drugs. Not only are young people needed to perform public services, but in performing these they may well find that their individual difficulties and confusions gradually disappear.

THE DRUG
CULTURE

FACTS AND FALLACIES

Much thought has been given to the significance of drugs in our society since the upsurge of drug use in the counter culture. The fact that the media have played up the mystique of psychedelic drugs among the young, together with youth's insistence that these drugs are an intrinsic part of their culture, has puzzled, frightened, and threatened the vast majority of adults — especially those unfamiliar with them. Yet we must not forget that America as a whole is actually a drug-oriented culture — and that *all* substances geared to reduce physical and/or psychological discomfort are drugs, whether they be aspirin, diet pills, sleeping pills, tranquilizers, alcohol, caffein, marijuana, or LSD. Some of these drugs are advertised and sold legally; some are not. *All* are potentially harmful.

Aside from those hallucinogenic drugs generally associated with the counter culture, Americans each year consume about twenty-seven million pounds of aspirin — enough to treat seventeen billion headaches. Four hundred tons of barbiturates are produced annually, a quantity that equals 3.6 billion normal doses. Approximately seventy million Americans drink alcohol regularly; and we do not really have to provide a statistical description of the massive consumption of cigarettes.

Aspirin, composed mostly of salicylate, affects almost every major system in the human organism. Depending on individual idiosyncracies and level of dosage, it can cause acute poisoning and even death. Barbiturates, the commonly used sedatives, are responsible for three thousand deaths a year due to accidental or intentional overdose. For millions of drinkers, alcohol has been related to personal disasters such as automobile accidents and divorce. Cigarette smoking has now definitely been found to be one of the factors in producing lung cancer, yet heavy smoking continues. And the use of these substances is *still* sanctioned by the law.

By quoting these statistics, we are not trying to urge that no drugs should be used because all are potentially dangerous, or that all drugs should be made freely available. Nor are we advocating stricter government measures on all substances. We are merely trying to point out that America is a drug-oriented culture and that youngsters who take drugs fall within a general pattern set by their parents. Young people differ and rebel only insofar as they use unsanctioned drugs or take unprescribed doses of legalized drugs.

Americans have traditionally turned to any substance or activity which promised rapid and easy solutions for problems. The use of drugs represents merely one aspect of this orientation. The orientation itself is perhaps an extension of our belief in technology, which presupposes that man can contrive substances that will easily relieve and better his condition. Whatever the reason, Americans have conventionally sought relief from pills. Generations of young people have been brought up with the notion that there is a chemical solution for any unpleasantness: physical, social, or psychological. Pills provide the cure for any ailment ranging from stomachache to personal anxiety, from nasal congestion to tension, from insomnia to failure in social or professional fields. Chemical concoctions provide us with an escape from the strains of interpersonal relations and the higher demands of our conscience; or they permit us to escape — like the "pep pills" — by immersing ourselves totally in work; or they relieve boredom.

The use of such drugs as marijuana, LSD, and even heroin by the young, then, is an outgrowth of a deeply rooted tradition that has become a problem in and of itself. Drug use is culturally symptomatic of our dependence on chemical substances to alter what are intrinsically social and psychological problems. On the individual level, heavy drug use is the expression and manifestation of personal difficulties. This is why, to use an extreme example, our heroin raids and treatment centers do not substantially affect the individual's heroin habit. To give a heroin addict methadone, or to imprison him, may rid him of the symptom of his illness, but it

110

does not relieve him of the disease of his life. It does nothing to alter his psychological makeup or social conditions. The person who turns to heavy drug use, whether it be constant marijuana use, taking frequent doses of amphetamines or barbiturates — or for that matter, alcohol — is turning to a substitute life style because his own is unsatisfactory. The problem generally lies in his life, not in his actual drug use, although clearly the abuse will become a problem in and of itself before long.

If the young are experimenting with or dependent upon mood and consciousness-altering drugs, they are telling us indirectly that, for some reason, they prefer a substitute life style to their actual one: that ersatz relations and experiences are more fulfilling, or more exciting, or more relevant to them than real ones.

Perhaps the facility with which they — as well as many of their parents — drift into this substitute life pattern is based on the prevalence of other forms of ersatz experience in our society, such as film and television. Having always lived at one remove from the wider range of sensations and happenings that television and film offer, the young find it easy and natural to continue this second-hand experience, this illusory existence, through the use of drugs. It is indeed psychologically contradictory that our society penalizes one form of ersatz behavior and encourages another.

Our cultural climate and psychological motivation for taking mood-altering drugs notwithstanding, one must not forget that tampering with chemical substances such as those most prevalent in the counter culture — marijuana, LSD, amphetamines, and barbiturates — can, with varying degrees of physical harm, have severe repercussions. Thus we must treat drugs, here, as a problem in themselves, for it is necessary that young people and adults alike be fully aware of the chemical constituents and effects of these substances. However, throughout our discussion it must never be forgotten that drug abuse is a symptom for an ailment or psychological difficulty, not the disease or the dilemma in itself.

TOBACCO

Many cultures have been confronted by an "underground" drug used by a relatively small section of the population for recreational or other reasons and condemned or prohibited by government and medical authorities, who attributed to the drug various kinds of

111

detrimental or magical potentials. In the seventeenth century the use of tobacco, then a new substance, was considered hazardous and outlawed in many countries. Penalties were severe. In Japan, the emperor forbade the planting and smoking of tobacco and there are records of at least one hundred and fifty people apprehended for buying and selling it, whose lives were in jeopardy. Violators in Persia were tortured and in some cases beheaded. The Mogul Emperor of Hindustan ordered that smokers' lips be slit. He ruled, "As the smoking of tobacco has taken a very bad effect in health and mind of so many persons, I order that no person shall practice the habit." The Czar of Russia forbade smoking in 1634. Both smokers and vendors were to suffer the penalty of having their lips slit and persistent violators were to be put to death. Medical reports of this period abound in details of the disastrous physical and mental effects of smoking.

TEA AND COFFEE

Tea and coffee have, in their day, similarly been viewed as malignant beverages. As late as the beginning of this century an English professor of physics together with a distinguished pharmacologist spoke of the dangers of excessive coffee consumption. In a standard medical textbook they wrote, "The sufferer is tremulous and loses his self command; he is subject to fits of agitation and depression. He has a haggard appearance . . . . As with other such agents, a renewed dose of the poison gives temporary relief, but at the cost of future misery." Tea was thought to be equally dangerous. "Tea has appeared to us to be especially efficient in producing nightmares with . . . hallucinations which may be alarming in their intensity . . . . Another peculiar quality of tea is to produce a strange and extreme degree of physical depression. An hour or two after breakfast at which tea has been taken . . . a grievous sinking . . . may seize upon the sufferer, so that to speak is an effort . . . . The speech may become weak and vague . . . . By miseries such as these, the best years of life may be spoilt."[1]

At the same time as this report on tea and coffee was written, the use of laudanum, a derivative of opium, was prevalent in England. It was recommended to old ladies for physical ills ranging from cough to cancer.

---

[1] Cannabis: British Report by the Advisory Committee on Drug Dependence, Longon, 1968, p. 16.

ALCOHOL

Perhaps the best known example of a drug prohibited by government is the 1919 National Prohibition amendment to the Constitution of the United States. While this amendment was in effect, the manufacture, sale, or transportation of any alcoholic beverage was considered illegal under federal law. Many people thus suffered severe penalties under a law which was repealed in 1933 as another amendment to the Constitution.

This historical perspective on various substances should warn us against making any dogmatic judgment against such drugs currently used by the young as marijuana. The plant, cannabis sativa, from which both hashish and marijuana are derived, has been in widespread use for centuries in such countries as India. The scare tactics which many parents as well as officials resort to are not the answer to the drug problem. Melodramatic descriptions of haggard marijuana users induced to crime often appear ridiculous in their historical context. As soon as a substance is accepted by a culture, permitted by law, its dramatic potential seems to be neutralized. Time has a tendency to cast that which is presently socially unacceptable into a different perspective.

Drugs and Youth

This is not to say that all contemporary drug use should be sanctioned by law. After all, the Russian Czar and Mogul Emperor have been proved correct in their judgment on cigarettes. But their penalties for smoking do appear more than a little severe, and one is led to wonder whether our own penalties for drug abuse will not seem equally barbaric a few decades from now. The young, whose experience with these drugs is greater than their parents', are well aware that very often the claims of the older generation have little basis in fact. Before a family dialogue on drugs can ensue, what is needed is an accurate estimate of the harmful possibilities of various drugs — which our modern chemical techniques permit us to estimate more definitively than in the past — and then a personal examination by both adults and the young of the reasons for using drugs.

We provide in the following pages an examination of the various drugs currently in use by the young; a fair estimate of their effect, the reasons for their use, and a description of the drug culture based on our personal research. We are not trying to tell any youngster to "turn off" if he smokes marijuana weekly, but we *are* suggesting that the answers to personal and social problems do not lie in drug use. The occasional marijuana cigarette may be a form of recreation, but frequent use intimates that there is a difficulty at hand which will not magically dissolve itself in a cloud of sweet-smelling smoke.

The information on drug use contained in this chapter is largely based on a National Institute of Mental Health-supported study of four hundred young people, divided into four groups: hippies, living in New York's East Village; those who take part in the hippie scene on weekends; those who do not take part in the hippie scene but who do use drugs; and those who neither affiliate themselves with hippies, nor take drugs. The population was composed of non-ghetto youth from the ages of thirteen to thirty. Conducted in and around the New York area in 1968 and 1969 by the Center for Community Research and a temporary staff of interviewers drawn from the adolescent and hippie population, the study gives us a factual basis for discussing the drug culture and provides us with the views of drug-using and "straight" youth. It is substantiated by more recent nation-wide studies on drug-using adolescents.

What Is a Hippie?

The term "hippie" should perhaps be defined for parents who tend mistakenly to associate any drug-using, long-haired adolescent with a "hippie." In our study, only those youngsters who met the following criteria were categorized as "hippies."
1. Self-perceived alienation from the goals and values of society.
2. Self-identification as "hippies" or "free men."
3. Identification and/or sympathy with a specific group of hippies, e.g., "diggers" or "provos."
4. A life style including dress and abode commonly associated with the hippies.
5. Identification with the drug scene.

Who Takes Drugs?

Hippies, of course, by definition. But drug use — and in our study we define a user as one who smokes marijuana one or more times a month — reaches far beyond the hippie group. One indication of

114

this is that we found it difficult to locate young people in the New York area, even among an exceedingly "straight" population, who could be clearly classified as non-drug users. If the present trend in drug usage is to continue, one could estimate that in the next ten years well over half of the population from the age of thirteen upwards will experiment with drugs.

From our study, we could describe hippies as youths who generally come from families in the middle-income bracket. This disputes the widely held view that hippies are the children of affluent professionals. Many of the hippies describe their childhood as being "unhappy" and they report that they overheard many arguments between their parents. The majority of our population of hippies come from broken homes and a background of family conflict and tension.

The non-hippie drug users in our sample come from a background which is financially upper class and made up of professionals and affluent businessmen — in other words, a background more affluent than that of either non-users or hippies. Their parental history is one of rapid social, vocational, and financial advancement. Sixty-two percent of these youths report happy childhoods and warm relations with their parents. These respondents are, for the most part, college students or professionals.

What our statistics on the educational status of non-hippie drug users suggest is that there is no direct relationship between recreational drug use and a history of adolescent dropping out or failure. Nor is there presently a direct connection between drug use and high intelligence, curiosity, and adventurousness, something which may have been true when drugs first started to be used. It can be said that recreational and occasional drug use has become so prevalent that one can no longer make distinctions of this kind.

What Are the Popular Drugs?

In order of preference, the drugs most commonly taken by the middle class youths represented in our study are marijuana (and hashish), LSD, amphetamines, and barbiturates. The young in our study show a great awareness of the properties of these drugs and the effects they can expect from them. In some cases, they stated that they would take whichever of the above drugs was available, but if all the drugs were available, they would choose a drug to fit the

115

state of mind they were in. Most of our respondents, however, chose marijuana and perhaps hashish, and only experimented occasionally with other drugs. The popular drugs are generally obtained from friends, and are rarely sold for a profit. While the males in our study reported that they often bought drugs, the females stated that drugs are most often given to them.

In the following description of the drugs most popular among our respondents, we will briefly review the history of each drug, its physical effects, the effects attributed to it by our study participants, and the hazards of abuse. As drugs are only one of the problems which arise between parents and adolescents, and as this book is about many other problems, no attempt is made to provide a comprehensive review of the vast literature on drugs, nor are all possible drugs included. We have included only those on which we have information from the subjects in our study. Parents and adolescents who are interested in more extensive information about drugs should send for the excellent series of Drug Information pamphlets developed by the Drug Abuse Section of the National Institute of Mental Health. These are available to the general public, without charge, by writing: National Clearinghouse for Drug Abuse Information; P.O. Box 1701; Washington, D.C. 20013.

THE AMPHETAMINES

Chemical and trade names: *Benzedrine, Dexadrine, Methadrine*

The amphetamines are stimulants known to millions of Americans as weight-reducing pills or pep pills taken by housewives, truck drivers, businessmen, and students for their ability to keep the user awake, active, and alert.

History of Amphetamine Use

Amphetamines were synthesized for medical purposes in 1927. It was noted that amphetamines could serve as a decongestant in the relief of cold symptoms because they shrink the nasal membranes. The benzedrine inhaler was introduced by Smith, Kline, and French in 1932. Further investigation revealed that the loss of appetite produced by the drug was helpful for weight reduction. The drug

116

also was found to counteract drowsiness. Physicians prescribe them to ward off fatigue during prolonged tasks. For instance, in World War II amphetamines were used to increase alertness among airmen flying long missions. The astronaut Gordon Cooper was ordered to take an amphetamine capsule to keep him alert, and to give him sharper reflexes when the ground controls failed during re-entry.

In the late 1930's students began to discover that amphetamines enabled them to stay awake for longer periods of time and to cram before exams. The drug soon was used by truck drivers and night watchmen to keep them awake for their work, and people from all walks of life began taking benzedrine as a "pick-me-up."

In 1965 laws were passed that gave the Food and Drug Administration authority to control the manufacture and distribution of amphetamines. These drugs are legally available only on a doctor's prescription.

Physical Effects

Amphetamines increase blood pressure; pulse, heart, respiratory, and metabolic rates. Appetite is decreased and the body is in a state of hyperalertness. Amphetamines produce a mood of tension and a generalized feeling of being keyed-up and ready for action.

Effects as Defined by Our Study Respondents

Our drug users state that they use amphetamines to help them to stay awake, to improve their studying potential, to ease depression, and to improve thinking. They also take amphetamines because they "provide a terrific feeling of being high, of soaring, of the greatest kicks."

The amphetamine high produces a feeling of well being or elation that is called being "up;" thus, the popular term for the amphetamines is "ups." The high is accompanied by feelings of power, self-confidence, and abundant energy. The sense of exhilaration created by amphetamines is very pleasurable to many.

Hazards of Usage

At this point the reader could well ask: "Why, if the effects of the drug are so pleasurable, if they produce exhilaration and a feeling of power, are they not available to the general public without a prescription?"

The body builds up a tolerance to the pills, so that increasingly larger doses are needed to maintain a high. By taking ever larger doses the user is not increasing his own energy; instead he is depleting the body's store of energy. When the effect of the pills wears off, the user may feel inordinately depressed and will require more pills to regain a feeling of well-being. Prolonged amphetamine use can lead to severe weight loss and can leave the user physically exhausted.

With continued use, psychological dependence is developed. The sense of power, self-confidence, and exhilaration are so compelling, and the fatigue and depression that follow upon discontinued use are so severe, that the temptation to resume use is very great. Adolescents, who are particularly prone to low feelings of self-esteem, are in danger of relying on this artificial and destructive means toward making them feel good about themselves.

Perhaps the greatest hazard lies in the possibility that the amphetamine user, in a never-ending search for more intense feelings of elation, will tire of taking mouthfuls of pills and begin to inject the drug directly into his veins. This process is known as "speeding" and the slogan SPEED KILLS, which made its way into the young drug-using population, speaks for itself. Taken intravenously, repeated reinjection can lead to complete physical exhaustion. Lack of food, sleep, and neglect of personal hygiene can lead to serious infections. At high dosages liver damage is possible and brain cell damage has also been reported.[1] Injected, "speed" gives the user an ecstatic high and an intense "rush" of energy which he can maintain only by continued injection. The depression which follows upon this particular high, known as the "crash," is extreme, and the desire to "feel normal again" usually necessitates further "shooting up." After a prolonged speed binge which may last four or five days, the individual is exhausted and may sleep continuously for two days. If the binge has been intense, suicidal depression may follow. Long-term heavy users can develop paranoid delusions and feelings of acute panic.

In our study, twice as many drug users report discontinued use as

---

[1] "Stimulants": United States Department of Health, Education and Welfare, Public Health Service Publication No. 2097.

report continued usage. In fact, when asked which of the various drugs they would not use again, the greatest single category of drugs chosen for disuse are the amphetamines. Thus, in spite of the reported pleasure produced by the drug, most of our respondents are acutely aware of its hazards and use the drug only occasionally or forego its use altogether.

COCAINE

Chemical or trade name: *Methylestor of benzoylecgonine*

Cocaine, a stimulant, is the bitter, crystalline alkaloid obtained from coca leaves (a shrub native to South America). It was once used in this country as a local anesthetic or a nerve block in surgery, but problems of habituation caused its manufacture and distribution to be carefully controlled. It is now available only by medical prescription.

History of Cocaine Use

The coca shrub has been extensively cultivated in Peru, and slightly cultivated over the entire South American continent since 1000 AD. The Incas first chewed coca leaves, symbolic of strength, endurance, and fertility, as an integral part of religious ceremonies. Early use was apparently confined to the court and nobility of the Inca Kingdom, but by the Spanish conquest (1532), its use was almost universal. By this time, use of the drug was not exclusively religious. It was used by the general populace, especially soldiers, to allay hunger, fatigue, and cold. It was also used as wages for native Indian labor, and as money by the Indians themselves. The high Andean people of Bolivia, Peru, and Colombia have been chewing coca leaves for centuries as a protection against their devastating living conditions. It is interesting to note that they give up the practice whenever they have occasion to journey to the more hospitable lowlands.

Coca was introduced medically into Europe in 1880, and at first heralded by Freud as a cure for morphinism. But the morphine addicts found it to be too much of a "welcome cure," and the drug was withdrawn from them. It was introduced into European society mainly by the upper classes, as they had access to the professional people who knew of its existence. In 1858 the active ingredient, cocaine, was isolated from coca, and use soon spread to the lower classes until the habit was causing alarm in Europe by the late 1800's.

The substance was introduced to the United States citizenry in commercial folk medicine and in some soft drinks, but in 1906 it was outlawed by the Pure Food and Drug Act, except through a doctor's prescription.

Physical Effects

Cocaine is a strong euphoriant, capable of producing feelings of sensual well-being, clarity, and excitement. Cocaine produces habituation, toxic effects, and drug dependency, but no physical addiction. After the "good feeling" wears off, the user is plagued with irritability, loss of appetite, and loss of sleep.

Hazards of Usage

While not physically addictive, an overdose of cocaine can be lethal, especially when purchased illegally. It is also the most expensive drug on the market.

BARBITURATES

Some trade names: *Phenobarbital, Amytal, Seconal, Nembutal, Luminal, Tuinal*

The barbiturates are commonly used in American homes as sedatives in order to induce sleep, to reduce anxiety, or to bring about a feeling of intoxication akin to that produced by alcohol.

History of Barbiturate Use

Barbiturates were first introduced into medicine in 1903. Their discovery was offered as a means of depressing the central nervous system to produce states ranging from mild sedation to deep

120

anesthesia. Today there are over fifty commercial brands on the market.

Barbiturates are generally classified in terms of duration of action as: (1) long-acting, (2) short-to-intermediate-acting, and (3) ultra-short-acting.

Barbiturates are controlled by the Comprehensive Drug Abuse Prevention and Control Act of 1970, so that they are available on prescription only. No prescription older than six months can be filled, and refills cannot be made more than five times in a six month period.

Physical Effects

Barbiturates act to depress and sedate the central nervous system. They act upon the cerebral centers and interfere with the passage of impulses in the brain. They relieve tension and anxiety. In larger doses they produce drowsiness and sleep.

Effects as Defined by Our Study Respondents

The respondents in our study state that they take barbiturates, or "downs," in order to relieve tension, "for kicks," or to "get high." Like others, they use "downs" in conjunction with amphetamines to counteract the depression that follows upon discontinued use of amphetamines. They are also taken in conjunction with alcohol to heighten the feeling of excitation or intoxication.

The high produced by barbiturates induces a feeling of dissociation or distance from the reality of problems. Thus, it creates the illusion of easing communication for self-conscious adolescents and stimulates a feeling of euphoria or heightened well-being.

Hazards of Usage

Within a very short period, regular use of barbiturates creates physiological dependence in the individual, and progressively greater quantities of the drug are needed to recreate the drug's original effects. Dosage quickly reaches a point where it exceeds the safe therapeutic level. The individual may then become accident-prone and confused. His mental ability and judgment are impaired; there is increased emotional instability and the risk of a sudden, perhaps lethal, overdose.

Every year there are approximately three thousand deaths due to accidental or intentional overdose of barbiturates. Accidental suicide occurs when sleeping pills are taken in order to produce sleep; if sleep does not follow, the individual may be confused and show poor judgment. He may then take further amounts which following on the first dose can produce death. In addition, normally non-lethal doses of barbiturates which follow ingestion of large amounts of alcohol may produce severe reactions. These drugs act to intensify each other's physical effects. They can depress heart action and breathing to the point where they cease.

Since they serve to produce a feeling of calm, people who are tense and anxious may become psychologically dependent. The need for increasingly large amounts to produce this feeling of calm, because of the rapid physical tolerance developed by the body, may cause death.

One further note about barbiturates is in order. Since they are used to produce a feeling of calm and to release tension, barbiturates are often confused with tranquilizers. However, tranquilizers can be used to counteract tension and anxiety without producing sleep. They should not be used in conjunction with alcohol.

THE HALLUCINOGENS

The psychedelic drugs, especially cannabis (marijuana and hashish), are those most widely used by, and associated with, the youth culture. These drugs evoke certain changes in the user's perception of himself, time, and space. Thus, they have been called mind-altering drugs, or, more technically, psychoactive drugs and hallucinogens. The psychedelics include such drugs as marijuana and hashish, LSD, psilocybin, mescaline and peyote. In this book we will describe only marijuana, and hashish, and LSD. Peyote, mescaline, and psilocybin are not as commonly used as LSD and since this is not intended to be a book about drugs only the briefest mention will be made of them here. In general, their effects are not as intense and dramatic as those obtained with LSD. Peyote, which derives from a cactus which grows in Mexico, and psilocybin, derived from a mushroom found also in Mexico, have both been used by primitive societies for divination and communion with supernatural powers. Little is known about the long-range effects or properties of any of these drugs. Persons interested in further information about these drugs are urged to write The National Institute of Mental Health or read Bernard Aaronson and Humphry

Osmond, *PSYCHEDELICS: The Uses and Implications of Hallucinogenic Drugs* (Doubleday, New York, 1970), in which a number of highly articulate professional people have richly described their experiences with these drugs.

CANNABIS
(Marijuana and Hashish)

History of Marijuana Use

Marijuana is derived from the common hemp plant, cannabis sativa, and is composed of the dried leaves and flowering shoots of the female plant. Hashish is a stronger form of cannabis and the substance is derived from the resin concentrated in the tops of the female plant. This resin, which is what contains the psychoactive chemical of the plant, is also found in lesser quantities in the leaves and shoots. Thus, the resin, hashish, is a great deal more potent than the tea-like leaves which constitute marijuana — the most widely used part of the cannabis plant in America. In effect, then, the majority of marijuana smoked in the United States is very weak and has very little and sometimes no hallucinogenic potential.

The properties of marijuana were documented in Chinese writings by 200 AD. The drug has been used for centuries throughout India, the Middle East, and in Africa.

As a medicine, marijuana has been used for various complaints such as pain, cough, rheumatism, asthma, and headaches. Other drugs have taken its place in modern medicine, so that it is no longer prescribed in the United States.

Marijuana is not a narcotic. Possession or dissemination of the drug is now classified as a misdemeanor instead of a felony, so that minimum mandatory penalties have been abolished. However, many state laws are more severe than federal law, dealing with marijuana as if it were a narcotic.

Physical Effects

The immediate effects include reddening of the whites of the eyes, and increased heart rate. The long-range effects of marijuana are unknown.

123

The psychological or subjective effects of marijuana, especially at the usual low dosage levels, depend to a large extent on the personality and mood of the user, the expectations he has been taught to have of the drug, and the circumstances under which he takes it. The same individual may have different experiences of marijuana at different times, and at the usual low-dosage levels these experiences are generally pleasurable.

Subjects in our study report that marijuana induces the following effects in them: relief of tension, intensification of perceptions, a feeling of elation, deepening of self-understanding, intensification of feelings, increase of creative potential, heightening of sexual experience, and facilitation of social experience. Marijuana is described as producing a feeling of inner contentment, a feeling of floating above reality, of exhilaration, of freely wandering imagination, and keen sense perception. It is perhaps not surprising that as so many positive effects are attributed to it, marijuana is the "drug of choice" among our study participants. It is especially interesting to compare their responses to marijuana and to alcohol. Alcohol is characterized by them primarily as a drug which relieves tensions and facilitates social experience. Alcohol does not have the myriad effects attributed to marijuana, e.g., intensification of feelings and perception, enhancement of creativity, deepening of self-understanding. Moreover, even in terms of major effects attributed to alcohol, i.e., tension relief and social facilitation, more subjects ascribe these effects to marijuana than to alcohol.

Users also report an alteration of their time and space sense in that minutes may seem to pass like hours and near objects may seem to be far away. Of all the drugs popular among the young, marijuana is the most social. Users rarely smoke on their own. It is a peer group experience and hence it is popular at parties. The cigarette or pipe passed around among friends is part of a social event. Our study findings tend to refute the myth of the pusher who starts his younger clients on marijuana in the hope of developing an older heroin client. In our study, the overwhelming majority of marijuana users "turn on" only previous users, generally their friends, and smoke with them in a social setting.

There are aspects of the adolescent as well as the adult marijuana mystique that need clarification. The widespread belief among the young that marijuana increases creativity has no basis in known fact. This is an illusion that is part of the "high" state, as are the immensely subjective judgments that marijuana increases self-understanding and fluency of articulation. The individual may feel this is the case, while high, but these feelings usually have no basis in reality outside the marijuana experience. The story of the individual who feels that he has been particularly witty during his last marijuana experience, only to be told by his non-smoking friend that he was a crashing bore, is all too common.

Public belief that marijuana smoking is related to sexual promiscuity is also highly dubious. It is true that marijuana may, like alcohol, relax the individual's inhibitions, if he wishes these to be relaxed, and may heighten the pleasure of the sexual experience, but there is no evidence that it encourages promiscuity. Indeed, many users claim that when they are high, they feel no need to engage in the added pleasure of sexual activity.

Hazards of Use

Marijuana is not a physically addictive substance. What is more usual is that the *heavy* smoker may develop a psychological dependence on marijuana and the feelings he believes it induces in him. He may use it as an escape from social or personal problems, but this, again, has more to do with the personality of the user than with the actual chemical properties of the substance. While some investigators have recently reported personality disturbances associated with marijuana use, these studies have been based on small numbers of psychiatric patients.

Investigation has not shown that the use of marijuana necessarily leads to the use of heavier drugs. Smoking marijuana bears no causal relation to heroin addiction, criminal behavior, traffic accidents, psychosis, gradual decline in working ability, or mental deterioration. There has been no definitive proof of long-term effects on the chronic user, though research studies on this issue are in process. The many social fears attributed to marijuana have no basis in currently known fact.

Since the effects of marijuana are so dependent on the mood and personality of the user, there are several things of which young smokers should be warned. Marijuana should never be smoked when one is anxious or depressed, and should not be pressed on an unwilling subject, since the user's mood and fear of drug effects or of possible legal action may be intensified during the experience (a "bad trip"). Secondly, and more significantly, adolescents should carefully calculate the personal implications of frequent marijuana use. Since the individual's suggestibility is increased under marijuana and since pressures are generally relieved, he may take part in actions which he would otherwise avoid; or he may find himself becoming increasingly apathetic to things he would normally care about.

It should of course be abundantly clear to any adolescent that parental concern about the possibility of arrest is legitimate. Therefore, it is the adolescent's responsibility, when this is a parental concern, to let his parents know that he knows enough not to smoke marijuana in public or in any other situation which is apt to bring about a confrontation with the law.

LYSERGIC ACID DIETHYLAMIDE (LSD)

History of LSD Use

LSD is a man-made drug first developed in 1938 from lysergic acid, one of the ergot alkaloids. Ergot is a fungus that grows as rust on rye. It was first used among experimental subjects under medical care. In the fifties a large number of investigators began to use it as a research tool. Some psychiatrists and psychologists are impressed with its ability to facilitate psychotherapy; others are not.

The use and distribution of the drug, since it has no proven medical value, is now illegal except by qualified investigators supported by the National Institute of Mental Health. This agency possesses the only legal supply of LSD in the United States. Research is being conducted to determine if the drug can be used in the treatment of alcoholism, emotional problems, and persons with terminal illness.

Physical Effects

The physical effects of LSD include enlarged pupils, flushed face, slight increase in blood pressure, a feeling of chill, and a possible slight increase in temperature and heart beat.

LSD acts on the central nervous system. It functions as a

126

stimulant to that part of the brain called the reticular formation. The stimulation of the reticular formation results in heightened sensitivity to stimuli from the external world received through the sense organs. This action causes distortion of what is perceived through the five senses. This is why a person under the effect of LSD can have his vision, hearing, taste, touch, and sense of smell temporarily altered.

Effects as Defined by Our Study Respondents

Though little is known of its definitive long-term physiological and psychological effects, the intensity, the heightened sense of meaning with which all that happens during the LSD trip is embued, has given the drug an aura of sanctity and ritual among the young.

Like marijuana, the effects of LSD are highly personal and depend on the user's expectations, mood, and setting. The most common effects reported during an eight-to-fourteen-hour LSD trip are: a deepening of self-understanding, intensification of perceptions, religious experience, and intensification of feelings. Though these effects may seem similar to those produced by marijuana, LSD causes much more potent reactions on the user's part.

Dramatic changes in perception are experienced, along with intensification and distortion of sense impressions. Colors, sounds, and textures may seem to be endowed with a rich life of their own and take on emotional significance. Often there is synesthesia — the sensation that one sensory experience is being translated into another. Thus, light can be heard or felt, sounds can be seen, music can be tasted. The walls surrounding the user may dissolve in a blaze of beautiful colors; he may feel he can think into and become a part of the scenes depicted in a painting hanging on the wall.

Users also frequently report a distortion of the body image so that part of the body may seem dramatically elongated or there is a sensation of dismemberment. The user may interpret this as amusing, strange, or terrifying.

During the eight to fourteen hours of the trip, there are usually extreme shifts in mood, which can range from calm, euphoria, and ecstasy, to depression, anxiety, and terror. Not only are rapid mood shifts possible, but individuals have described experiences of contradictory emotions co-existing simultaneously. Thus joy and sadness, loneliness and intimacy, love and hate, may all co-exist.

127

Thoughts seem to move more rapidly, and past, present, and future may become confused. Abstract thinking may be impaired and there is often a dream-like blending of the boundaries between conscious and unconscious. Some users seem to have an acute awareness of the fact that the effects they are experiencing are due to the drug; among others true hallucinations do occur. For example, many users know that the wall dissolving with colors is an effect produced by the drug, and would therefore not be hallucinating; other users might believe the walls were really dissolving — a true hallucination.

Many subjects report a heightened sense of self-awareness. Long forgotten trivial memories may be vividly recalled and experienced as if they were being actually lived in the present. Others experience a rapid alteration in self-image. They feel as if they were a number of different selves, and they react to these different self images alternately with pride, guilt, delight, and sadness. Often the individual is convinced that he is seeing himself for the first time as he really is. One of the most common statements is that the drug "helps me get inside my head."

While there is no evidence to support the user's conviction that life has taken on greater meaning, that he has become more creative, and that self-awareness has increased, these convictions are experienced by the user with such intensity that he believes in their factual status.

Hazards of LSD Use

In some users there is a recurrence of the features of the LSD state months after the last dose. This phenomenon, known as "flashback," can cause terror to the user who feels it is not within his control and who thus fears that he is going crazy.

The intensity of the experiences during an LSD trip can cause feelings of acute panic in the user. The user may experience visual distortions so intense that he "sees" the very walls closing in on him, and his body changing into some dreadfully deformed shape. Terrifying experiences of this kind are known by users as a "bad trip." Unfortunately there is no way to predict who will have a good or bad trip; a number of previous good trips is no guarantee that the next one will not be filled with terror and horror.

The dangers of LSD, apart from the possibility of bad trips and flashbacks, lie largely in the fact that its effects can have very serious consequences. There is little doubt that, in susceptible persons, LSD can play a role in bringing about acute and sometimes long-lasting mental illness, requiring hospitalization. In some instances, the panic produced by the drug or the feeling of invincible power has resulted in suicide and death due to a disregard for ordinary personal safety. In addition, some investigators have found evidence of chromosome breakdown, although others have not. It has not been proven that such breaks cause birth defects. However, given our present knowledge coupled with the potency of the drug, use of LSD is at best hazardous.

There is a further danger involved in LSD's illegality, since users are never fully aware of the dosage level and the purity of the substance they are taking. Thus stronger effects than desired or expected can occur; and there is a possibility of other toxic substances, notably amphetamines, being present in the black market drug. Severe panic due to a strong dose, and feelings of invulnerability that result in great risk or death, have been reported.

LSD is not known to be physiologically addictive, but users can become dependent on the psychological effects of the drug. The young are aware of these dangers, and there seems to have been a decline in the use of LSD over the last few years. Experimentation with the drug still occurs, but this, amongst most adolescents, is usually limited to a short period of time or to infrequent trips. The sanctity of LSD as a sacrament in the anti-establishment religion seems to have declined.

THE NARCOTICS

The term *narcotic* refers to opium and pain-killing drugs made from opium, such as heroin, morphine, and codeine. In this book we will describe only the most commonly used of these drugs, heroin.

History of Heroin Use

Heroin is actually a man-made derivative of morphine, and was first used as a substitute for morphine addiction. Originally, physicians thought heroin to be a non-addicting cure for morphine addiction. They soon discovered heroin to be highly addictive.

Heroin is far more potent than morphine, shorter acting, and

129

more rapid in onset. Medically it has no advantage over morphine; and, unlike morphine, its manufacture and trade are illegal in the United States.

Physical Effects

The drug depresses certain areas of the brain, and tends to reduce hunger, thirst, and sexual desires.

Effects as Defined by Our Study Respondents

Heroin gives the user the impression that he is carefree, that he has no worries or tensions. The drug induces a "rush" which is characterized by feelings of tranquility and euphoria. Following the initial effects of the narcotic, users "go on the nod," a dreamy state of utter non-caring.

Heroin is used by middle class adolescents out of curiosity and a desire to experience the "high" produced by the drug. Among our subjects it is not a drug of choice and no one had used it more than a few times. Generally, the effects produced by marijuana and LSD are of much greater appeal and interest to our study respondents.

Hazards of Heroin Use

The hazards of heroin use are very serious. One of the hazards is that the user can never be sure of the strength of the dose he is taking, so that undesirable effects from vomiting to respiratory depression and death can occur.

Heroin users usually begin by sniffing or "snorting" the powder. They then commonly progress to intravenous injection. The addict's equipment generally consists of matches, a medicine dropper, a teaspoon with a bent handle in which the dissolved powder is heated, a piece of cotton through which it is filtered, and a hypodermic needle with which the "fix" is administered directly into a vein. This process is known as "mainlining," and its inherent dangers are blood poisoning, tetanus, hepatitis, and the lethal overdose.

Physiologically, heroin is a highly addictive drug. The user quickly builds up a tolerance for it and requires increasingly larger doses in order to maintain a high and to avoid the physical agony of withdrawal. Addicts are forced to spend inordinate sums of money in order to maintain their habit. It is in an effort to maintain this increasingly expensive habit that so many users resort to criminal activities.

The psychological danger of heroin addiction is that the individual's entire life becomes centered around his habit. All activities are performed in expectation of the next fix and one fix leads necessarily to another in an endless round of trying to stave off the depression which follows upon euphoria and the need to get high once again. The addict's pattern is one of escape from the realities of ordinary life.

Adolescents who use heroin out of curiosity or to see if they can "beat the habit" should know that they are flirting with an extremely dangerous drug. The notion that, as long as heroin is only snorted or injected just under the skin it is not addictive, is simply not true.

Why Does Youth Turn to Drugs?

An overwhelming majority of the youngsters we interviewed state that they tried drugs out of curiosity, a sense of experimentation, or merely out of boredom: there just wasn't anything else meaningful to do. They wanted to experience the feeling of being "high" they had heard so much about. Contrary to what many adults may think about the reasons for drug use, these youngsters were undergoing no great internal problems or external conflicts at the time of their first drug experience, though of course, like everyone else, they had some problems. They turned to drugs, especially marijuana, for relaxation or entertainment. Only ten percent of these youngsters state that they were feeling miserable when they first took drugs. These statistics should suggest to parents that finding a little marijuana in any adolescent's drawer does not warrant a trip to a psychiatrist. Most of the time drugs are taken for pleasure or, with some of the psychedelics, in an attempt to deepen self-understanding. While one in every seven subjects do see drug use as a means of dealing with personal problems, the commonsensical attitude on the part of the overwhelming majority of youth is something parents should take into consideration before they alienate their youngster by reacting hysterically to what may be a very casual use of drugs.

What Are the Problems Young People Confront?

The problems of the young people described in our study are feelings of detachment from society, a lack of meaning and direction in life, and a lack of attachment to one person. Thirty-seven percent of the non-hippie drug users interviewed report some feelings of sadness and tension; twenty-six percent state that they were having difficulty in getting along with their family; twenty-three percent were experiencing trouble in relation to friends; and twenty-one percent report that they were experiencing difficulties in school. It is to these root problems that parents should direct their attention rather than to what is in most cases the secondary issue of drugs.

How Does Youth See Itself and the Rest of the World?

Our study of hippies and non-hippies points to a practical reaffirmation of our earlier discussion of the counter culture. Forty-six percent of the 200 non-hippies (100 drug users and 100 non-users) in our sample see themselves as outsiders to traditional middle class institutions, 35 percent see themselves as outsiders to the age of technology, and 24 percent see themselves as outsiders to contemporary America. While these percentages are higher among drug users they are still very high when the non-users are considered alone. If we remember that many of these youngsters have excellent school records and in many cases a history of active participation and even leadership in school activities, then one is led to conclude that the most promising sector of American youth is thoroughly disenchanted with the status quo.

The majority of these young drug users state that they feel positively about their parents, but this does not diminish their sense of "apartness" from the family. Though they like their parents, 84% of the non-hippie drug users and 67% of the non-users state that they feel that most parents "mess up their kids." Furthermore, only 48% of the users and 60% of the non-users envisage future success for themselves in the working world. Many claim that work is a "bore," a "middle-class hangup," or a "necessary evil." The established modes of achievement do not interest them.

Much has already been said about the alienation of contemporary youth. Nevertheless, it is still interesting to see the figures we have gathered to support this, for they give a palpable reality to the abstraction. What is particularly noteworthy about our findings is that they show that drug-taking youths are not alone in confessing to feelings of alienation. Discontent seems to be a common element of our youthful population, and though drug users may stress various aspects of alienation more strongly, the difference between them and non-drug-taking youth is one of degree rather than of kind. Fifty-one percent of our drug users and 31% of non-users (i.e., one out of every three) feel that the schools are becoming more and more irrelevant. In response to the statement: "In government today there is no one you can really trust," the vast majority of the users as well as non-users agree with the statement. Two out of four feel that it is unimportant to make a great deal of money and to attain any kind of professional status. This confirms our analysis concerning the inward orientation of large segments of contemporary youth. More strikingly still, one-third of these youngsters say that they would like to emigrate to another country and 42% of the users and 14% of the non-users state directly that they feel alienated from society. The figures on all these issues are considerably higher for the hippies. The non-hippies when compared to the hippies differ significantly on most measures of alienation. Nevertheless, when the data on the non-hippies, both users and non-users, are examined in their own right, it becomes clear that many of these youth are also disaffected and disenchanted. To the extent that they are in some ways representative of urban and suburban youth, it is apparent that there is considerable discontent among "ordinary" youth. Certainly this discontent is not restricted to the hippies. Perhaps the historical role of the hippies has been to catalyze, crystallize, and embody the malaise of a generation.

It is extremely important for parents to note that this chronic air of discontent among the young is not a concomitant of drug use. There is no evidence to suggest that the taking of drugs leads to a greater feeling of alienation, confusion, or disillusionment, but rather drug use is merely another expression of this alienation. There has been a disproportionate emphasis on the determining place of drugs in the lives of our young. This is made clear by the fact that when our sample drug users were asked what event had most affected their recent lives, none of them mention the drug experience. Rather, they include such events as beginning to work, leaving school, and moving away from home. Another feature that points to the secondary importance of drugs in the lives of these young drug users (and it should be noted that we are not speaking here of abusers) is that they do not necessarily seek out drug-using friends or even value this feature in friends. An overwhelming proportion of the young we interviewed state that they value honesty and loyalty in friends above all else. Drug use as an attribute in a friend is scarcely ever mentioned. This suggests that drug-using youth do not stress the place of drugs in their lives to the extent that their parents and media critics do.

It is interesting to note that in the face of the rather widespread disenchantment with accepted values, very few of the young people in our sample chose to classify themselves as radicals or affiliates of the New Left when they were questioned about their political leanings. The hippies are proportionately more radical, followed by drug users, and, not too far behind, non-drug users. The breakdown is as follows: in the total sample, 27% define themselves as radical, 18% as New Left, and 21% as liberal; thus, 66% define themselves as left of center. Only seven percent of the total sample see themselves as conservative. Although many of the young, drug users and non-drug users alike, do not define themselves as radicals, they still tend toward a radical critique of our present system. In the face of the disillusionment which has followed upon our involvement in South East Asia, this is not surprising.

What Are Young People's Attitudes toward Sex and Marriage?

Regarding sex and marriage, we find that the views of hippies and drug-using youth are once again more radical than the views of "straight" youth. However, here too, the difference is one of degree, not of kind, and is as great between hippies and drug users as between drug users and non-drug users. Our evidence suggests that non-hippie drug users are not significantly more permissive in their attitude toward sex than non-drug-using youth. But it does clearly point to the fact that the young have in many instances rebelled against traditional moral codes.

Approximately 70% of the non-hippie youngsters in our sample feel that there is nothing wrong with premarital sex. Among non-drug users this figure is slightly lower, but still 60%. While subjects in all our groups question the sanctity of marriage, nevertheless a majority of all non-hippies agree with the statement "Getting married is important to me." Similarly, while premarital sex is accepted by the great majority of all respondents, extramarital sex is accepted by a minority, even among the hippies.

No one strongly disagrees with the statement: "Laws regulating sexual practices should be abolished," thereby intimating that the young believe sex to be a private matter left up to the individual conscience. Similarly, 70% of the non-drug users agree that "Abortions should be legal," and 89% of the subjects in this group agree with the statement that "Teenagers should be given access to information about contraception."

Though these views would seem to convey the idea that the young have abandoned their elders' morality and have accepted a more permissive way of life, the double standard for men and women is still very much in evidence among non-hippie youth. Forty percent of non-drug users and 24% of users agree with the statement: "I don't respect girls who sleep around." Only 24% of non-users and 11% of users say that they don't "respect guys who sleep around." This suggests that the new permissiveness still favors men over women.

Why Do Drug Users Stop Taking Drugs?

We have found in our experience with adolescents that frequently there is a two-year period — generally during the high school years — in which youngsters experiment with drugs. Then experimentation ceases in most cases, and the adolescent may turn his interest to other areas, though still occasionally smoking the marijuana cigarette offered to him. The young state that they stop using drugs because they lose interest or because they fear physical damage from extended use of certain drugs. Some say they stop because they have consistently experienced "bad trips." Others feel that they need their "head," their intellect, in order to change society.

It is not surprising that in this age of rapid change the adolescent's interests should change equally rapidly. Thus, the drugs which were initially taken for entertainment value, out of curiosity, or in an attempt to relieve boredom, can themselves become boring. It is almost as if, in most cases, the adolescent outgrows experimentation with drugs as he outgrows his social and sexual awkwardness. Often the necessity to do well in college or to hold a job will leave him little time for drug-oriented recreation. The healthy youngster will generally realize that he needs his head more than he needs drug-induced sensations. It is usually only when the youngster has gone to drugs in an attempt to escape personal problems and has developed a totally drug-oriented existence that this loss of interest does not take place.

Some Final Thoughts

Though the use of illegal drugs may symbolize youth's rebellion against the establishment, we have seen in this chapter that drug use is in most cases neither the cause nor the result of youth's discontent with contemporary society. The young may champion psychedelic drugs precisely because of their illegality, since the establishment's frenzied claims about such seemingly harmless drugs as marijuana pinpoint its prejudices and the distortion of truth which extends to many other issues. They may turn to these drugs for entertainment, out of curiosity, or because they feel that these drugs will provide them with those introspective possibilities that our externally and materially oriented world negates. They may simply take drugs because it is an experience which identifies their generation and links each individual to a wider and more flexible social group. However, in relatively few cases do they seek in drugs the solution to personal problems. It is only when and if they do that the question of drug dependence becomes relevant.

When drugs seem to provide an escape from or an answer to an otherwise apparently impossible life, it is then that the individual and his family must take a close look at their respective positions and attempt, perhaps with outside help, to remedy the situation. Heavy use of even the most apparently harmless drugs, such as marijuana, suggests that the individual's life has become centered on drugs and that he is substituting an artificial form of existence for realities he cannot face. In many communities across the nation there are clinics and special associations which provide counselling and treatment facilities for young abusers and their families. Parents and adolescents are urged to assess honestly and rationally whether there is a problem and if so to seek professional help in their community. Referrals for treatment may be obtained through contacting county and state Mental Health Boards.

If we stress that there are relatively "healthy" ways of using drugs as well as unhealthy or dangerous ones, this does not mean that we condone the use of illegal drugs. Every youngster as well as his parents must be aware of the repercussions of performing an illegal act. Since the penalties for drug use differ in every state of the union, we have not presented them here; parents and adolescents who want information on this topic can call their county legal officer or local District Attorney. The attempt to expand consciousness, attain self-knowledge, or have religious experiences by means of drugs is highly questionable. There is no quick and easy road to any of these things. Finally, the possibility of increased suggestibility with drug use, or an apathetic reaction to the world outside drugs, is socially hazardous in our contemporary world, where every individual is needed to play a role in determining society's course. These are matters which every adolescent must consider carefully.

On the other hand, our statistics show that youngsters who take drugs casually or for recreational purposes constitute an intelligent and aware sector of the adolescent population. Thus, parents are cautioned not to react hysterically if they discover that their youngsters smoke marijuana occasionally. What is required here, as in other cases, is a discussion of the reasons for drug use, a clear definition of the dangers of use, and an understanding by the young that there are many aspects of life that provide an alternative to immersion in the drug culture. For many youngsters these days, taking drugs seems to be a part of growing up, just as is making love or seeing friends; but it is still important for the teenager as well as the parent to ask how the drugs are being taken, when, and why, so that the road to a self-destructive use of drugs is barred.

It should be noted that, because of the possibility of panic reactions, it is extremely important to avoid alarming, confusing, or upsetting a person who is under the influence of *any* drug. Therefore, however difficult this might be, it is critical to act in a reassuring manner until the effects of the drug have worn off. It is only at that time that any conversation about drug use can — and should — begin.

Finally, every youngster who is dissatisfied with the status quo and wishes to change social and human conditions should think seriously of the fate of a society that seeks pleasure or quietude in mood-altering drugs. George Orwell's vision of a totalitarian society in which "Big Brother" watches over and conditions his subjects by means of chemical substances designed to keep them in a subdued state of detached euphoria should warn us that 1984 may not be too many years away. The drugs used initially as a form of rebellion against the establishment can easily — if the young desire them enough and are not watchful — be legalized and exploited by authority to control any further possibilities of rebellion and criticism.

THE ART OF
THE DIALOGUE

NEGATIVE TACTICS
VS
POSITIVE DIALOGUES

We have explored the cultural and environmental terrain separating contemporary parents and teenagers. The issues discussed in the preceding pages find their echo in many instances of familial strife. Drug-use, sexual permissiveness, political views, the rejection of work in favor of pleasure, length of hair, and adolescent dress, all weave their way into the family and in various forms become the basis of hostility.

However, differences in outlook and in values need not necessarily result either in the total breakdown of communication between the generations or in lightly veiled warfare. Adolescents, as well as adults, want affection, trust, and respect for their separate identity, especially from those closest to them; often when these are lacking, mutual misunderstanding results in the family. Points of contention between the generations can be handled in a manner which breeds harmony rather than distrust or hostility. This is not to say that all tensions can be erased, since tension often seems to be an essential part of the growth process and of cohabitation. Fortunately, there are ways of confronting differences in outlook or opinion that initiate greater understanding.

In this chapter we turn from the culture to the individual. We

141

shall describe several often-found patterns of attitudes and behaviors on the part of both parents and teenagers that promote friction in the family.

Since talk is our primary mode of expression, it is probably the best way in which understanding can be brought about in the family. Therefore, we will designate negative or tension-causing attitudes and then provide "model" dialogues which relate to several key instances of familial conflict. However, the teenager often interprets the tone of the put-down along with its content and sees it as a direct denigration of himself and of many aspects of his existence. Jeans, for example, may be the trademark of his particular generation or group, and may be associated with a certain life style. The teenager may take pride in this group or in the particular crease of his jeans. In any case, his need for approval is severely jeopardized by the put-down tactic, which can only be reacted to with hostility, or a stubborn defense of what has, because of the comment, become an entrenched position. These dialogues are not intended for memorization and regurgitation; rather, they provide hints as to how tension-provoking situations, familiar to all parents and teenagers, can be handled so that a permanent, open-ended dialogue of trust can be set up between the generations.

The "Put-Down"

The "put-down" tactic is one in which both parents and adolescents often indulge. Frequently it provides a true, but negative, expression of sentiment. While sometimes it is unconsciously insulting, at other times it is calculated to hurt. The put-down is primarily an explosion of long-repressed hostility.

As an example of the first, we can see a mother — much like the well-meaning mother of Anna in our first profile — who greets her child with the exclamation "Oh, you look awful. Do you have to wear those grimy jeans every day?" not realizing that her daughter, despite the jeans, has taken some care with her appearance. This type of put-down comment can extend to long hair, beards, or even "that awful-looking person I saw you with." Parents are often unaware of their adolescent's sensitivity regarding every aspect of their appearance, as well as those of their friends. They do not intend to insult, but feel they are offering a well-founded evaluation.

It may seem a little ridiculous to elevate jeans or appearances to such a place of importance. But our experience has shown us that it is precisely such minor matters and put-downs that in the long run result in family hostility and the breakdown of understanding. It is because of the frequency of such unconscious exclamations that teenagers often feel they are being hassled by their parents. Further, though the question of appearances may seem to be a minor one, it is in fact only termed "superficial" to the person who is being accused. "Oh Mom, you just don't want me to wear jeans because you're worried about what the neighbors will think," mirrors the teenager's resentment of his mother's superficiality. But the knife is double-edged. The teenager often wishes to wear jeans or his hair long precisely because this makes him acceptable to his fellows. Neither attitude is superficial in itself, since we are all concerned with the impression we and those closest to us make on the world around us.

When a "put-down" occurs in a family situation, the victim of the slight should attempt to realize that what is being said is not a total and irrevocable judgment on his individuality. The mother's "Oh, you look awful" is not usually her ultimate or even general estimate of the child, and before reacting too strongly, the teenager should pause and remember this. Given the natural human inability to distance oneself at the moment of attack, however, this is extremely difficult to do. Therefore, it is far better that all members of the family refrain from this kind of tactic. The teenager will not do better in his schoolwork, nor will he be willing to alter his appearance or life style if he is told, "Oh, you'll never amount to anything. You're impossible!" Or, "I'm ashamed to be seen with you in public." Adolescent individuality is a frail thing and cannot be handled in this way if parents expect positive results from their children.

Let us suppose that a mother really objects to her daughter's constant wearing of jeans. How can this situation be handled *reasonably?* (The same kind of approach can apply to many situations which generally provoke put-downs: appearance, schoolwork, objection to a particular friend, etc.)

MOTHER: Kate, must you wear jeans all the time?
DAUGHTER: But Mom, all the kids do. I don't tell you what to wear, do I?

MOTHER: Oh Kate, you do look so much better in a dress and I really dislike jeans.

DAUGHTER: Why? You're only worried about what your friends will think. It's true that they'd look pretty awful in jeans.

MOTHER: (*laughing*) I guess you're half right about that. But tell me, don't you get bored just wearing the same thing all the time?

DAUGHTER: (*shrugging*) Mom, I told you. All the kids wear them. I can't go around wearing fancy things. I'd stick out like a sore thumb. Imagine if you wore jeans to a cocktail party. That's the same as my wearing a frilly dress to go to school, or even to a movie.

MOTHER: Well, I'm still not crazy about you in jeans, but I understand what you're telling me. I think you're saying that right now this is the style of dress of your friends and that this is what makes it appropriate. But that means in another group, with a different style of dress, another outfit would be appropriate. So can we agree that you won't wear jeans when my friends come over or when we go out with the family? How's that?

DAUGHTER: That's fine, Mom.

MOTHER: O.K. I won't bother you about it again.

Mutual explanation of positions leading toward understanding is the key. Put-downs are unnecessary since neither side can win or lose in the generational struggle, if hostility in the family is aggravated. But a form of compromise can be entered upon. We have found that often, when familial tension is especially high, a contract drawn up between parents and adolescents in the presence of a third party, an objective mediator, can be useful. For example: if mother and daughter cannot arrive at this compromise on their own, sometimes another relative or friend of either one can be a great help in clarifying the basic issues. A reasoned compromise of this sort can make life in the family much more agreeable.

Teenagers, too, are guilty of put-downs. These are often of the harsher sort emerging from repressed hostility, and they are calculated to hurt. Many are the parents in our files who have been told, "You've never done anything useful in your whole life. All you're interested in is making money. You don't care about all the suffering that goes on around us." And many are the parents

144

who have risen to the attack by tallying: "Well, I don't see you giving up the comforts I've provided for you. You still use the car, watch your *own* television set . . . " The trouble with the put-down tactic as a way of expressing criticism is that it prohibits any further communication and creates scars which can only result in resentment or enmity.

A teenager who really feels strongly about his father's seeming lack of concern about social ills — and is not merely lashing out — should try to explain to him what he believes can and must be done. The wise father will listen willingly, without flaring up and jumping to his own defense, before explaining his own position. Above all, he should not react to this criticism as if it were an overt challenge to his authority or a threat. The following provides a possible alternative to this type of deeply hostile put-down, together with a possible means of responding.

SON: Oh God, Dad. Don't you ever think about anything except making money?

FATHER: I guess it just seems that way to you, John. You know, it's not that easy for me to send you and your sisters through college. Nevertheless, I do occasionally think about other things.

SON: Yeah? Like what?

FATHER: Well, I'm concerned about our community and the way things seem to be going down hill.

SON: Well, there are more important things going on, like the war in Vietnam and Laos . . . racial tension . . . poverty in the cities . . . pollution. My God, Dad, the whole world is in chaos.

FATHER: Well, you're right. I guess I don't spend my days worrying about it. But you should know by now that I don't agree with this war. Tell you what, if you can show me what I could possibly do about it, I promise to give it some serious thought.

This type of dialogue leaves the way open to further communication between father and son, rather than creating a barrier of hostility between adolescent and adult. It attempts to create understanding by focusing not on what separates father and son, but rather on those views they hold in common. Concentration on shared points and not on differences is necessary if young people and adults are to communicate in a manner that will enable them to learn and live together.

What must be remembered about the put-down is that it often constitutes an expression of anger or criticism. Neither of these are necessarily destructive of relationships in their own right. It is far better to express anger than to repress it and allow tension to build up to an exploding point. But the anger, if one wishes to create good parent-teenager relationships, must be channeled at the situation at hand, not at the person in question. For example, the mother who is furious at her daughter for showing herself wearing jeans in front of her bridge friends should not lash out with a personalized put-down, "Oh, you look awful. You put me to shame." Instead she might find a release for her anger by saying, "It really upsets me to have you wearing dirty jeans in front of my friends. I really wish you wouldn't." She may find that her daughter has taken her feelings into consideration and appears wearing a dress on the next occasion.

Criticism, too, is often necessary. But it is only constructive if it is directed at the wrongs of a situation rather than at those of the individual. The teenager who brings home a far from ideal report card is not helped in any way if he is told that he is stupid and will never amount to anything. However, if his father sits down with him and says, "I see you've failed math and chemistry. Perhaps you need extra tutoring in these two subjects," the condition is being tackled rather than the individual attacked. Father and son can arrive at a way of altering the situation and the youngster's self-esteem is not hopelessly shattered. In all cases, whether it be the matter of personal appearance, a sloppy room, poor grades, or constant lateness for dinner or school, personal attacks are pointless, and can only lead to greater friction. Criticism is only constructive when it focuses on the condition at hand, not at the totality of the person.

Guilt: Personal Association and Past History

Though they often hesitate to admit it, parents at times resent the fact that they have spent so much time and effort in bringing up children who seem to be either indifferent to them, ungrateful, or openly hostile. They are further indignant that their children have not turned out as they might have wished, and they express their exasperation or unconscious resentment by making guilt-provoking statements. We have heard many mothers and fathers

146

make such apparently casual remarks to their child as, "Oh, you're turning out to be just another hippie." Or, "After all I've done for you, after the way I've brought you up, all you can do is run around with that no-good crowd of dropouts." Or, "You repay my love by playing around with that obnoxious boyfriend of yours."

Parents often do not realize how this kind of statement can antagonize the adolescent. No one likes to be reminded of one's unfulfilled obligations, nor of how much has been done for one. Furthermore, by disparaging the adolescent's friends or the group he appears to be in contact with, one is necessarily disparaging him. Teenagers, who often are confronted by such remarks, can only react out of a momentary hatred for the parent-assailant and retaliate with, "You should take a look at *your* friends someday. They're just a stupid, narrow-minded lot." Or, "Why did you have me in the first place? I didn't ask to be put into the world. You could have saved yourself a lot of money and trouble!"

Adolescents engage in similar guilt-producing comments directed at their parents by associating their elders with what they consider a negligible faction of society. "Oh Mom, what do you know? You're just an ordinary housewife." Or, "Dad, what can you understand about my life? You're just like all the rest of those limited businessmen." This is a put-down tactic, but it can also bring guilt feelings on the parents' part if the adolescent has sensed that his parent is a little defensive or sensitive about his role in the world. The only thing which can result from such guilt-provoking repartee is silent rage or a full-scale familial battle. Both parents and adolescents, in the interest of family harmony, should try to refrain from taking this kind of stand.

Another form of guilt-attributing and guilt-producing mode of expression consists of comments that judge the individual guilty by reminding him of some act he has committed in the past. For example: Father to son — "How can I allow you to go to the country for the weekend? Last time you went, you didn't call home the entire time, and we were worried sick. Then, when you finally got back, I found the car fender dented. Really, Johnny, I can't trust you." This kind of statement necessarily evokes a feeling of guilt and hostility on the adolescent's part, since some long-forgotten mishap is thrust into the present and his sense of responsibility is undermined. If the parent feels that he does not want his teenager to undertake any particular activity, it is far better that he find reasons valid in the present for not doing whatever is at hand. The wise father will point out that his son has been out with his friends three weekends in a row, that he has a lot of school work to complete, and that his parents would sincerely like to have him around to talk to for a change.

Teenagers, too, often bring up past misadventures calculated to evoke guilt feelings when they wish their parents to refrain from doing something. A comment made in various ways by many adolescent girls comes to mind here. "Oh Mom, I don't want you to come and sit with my friends when they're over here. Last time, you sat there and talked all the time about silly things and were trying to act like a teenager. You made both of us look foolish."

Parents should realize that teenagers often regard their presence amongst their friends as intrusive, and designed to make them feel uncomfortable. However, it is up to the adolescent to explain why this is so to the parents, without offending them. A young girl confronted by such a situation could tell her mother that she and her friends wish to be alone since they have things to discuss which only interest them. Her mother can come in for a little while, but her friends will only be made uncomfortable if she stays on too long. Tact is necessary in all these matters, for family harmony is a delicate state, too easily shattered by guilt-inducing statements.

Let us imagine a common situation involving mother and daughter in which the parent might most naturally resort to a guilt-provoking comment. The mother has just discovered some contraceptive pills in her daughter's drawer. She is deeply upset by what she considers to be a secret and perhaps perverse or dangerous existence on her daughter's part, and her first reaction is to seek out her daughter and exclaim, "Debbie, how could you do this to me! After all I've taught you and all the trust I've placed in you. How can you go around sleeping with men behind my back? Is this how you repay my love?"

This statement may sound exaggerated on the printed page, but within the family, it occurs all too often. The only kind of comment it can be countered with is the daughter's, "Oh Mom, you're being silly. I haven't done anything to you and I don't want to discuss it. I'm a big girl now, you know." This precludes the possibility of any fruitful communication taking place, and the mother has lost a valuable opportunity for discussing important matters with her daughter. If the mother is truly upset and wishes to discuss the subject of sex seriously with her child, then there are ways of promoting a hostility-free interchange.

MOTHER: *(gently)* Debbie, I've found these pills in your drawer. I'm surprised that you haven't wanted to tell me about this before.

DEBBIE: Oh Mom. It's a personal thing. Anyhow, I thought you'd be angry and wouldn't understand.

MOTHER: Well, I can't say I'm exactly overjoyed. But if it's already happened, I'd like to talk about it.

DEBBIE: *(relieved)* O.K., Mom.

MOTHER: Would you like to tell me about it?

DEBBIE: Well, I've been going with Mike and that's part of our relationship.

MOTHER: The one thing I absolutely don't want you to get involved in — because it's unwise and can only hurt you — is a round of casual relationships that involve sex. Believe me, Debbie, I know what I'm talking about. It's so easy in these days of contraceptive pills to treat making love as loosely as a handshake. And that's dangerous — not because of the possibility of pregnancy, which still exists — but because of what it can do to you as a person.

DEBBIE: But times have changed, Mom. I'm not going to make love to only one man for the whole of my life. Why, all the girls . . .

MOTHER: Debbie, I don't care about all the girls. You're you, and you have only yourself to account for. Times may have changed, but women and their emotions haven't changed all that much. And I want you to think carefully if the relationship you're involved in is purely sexual, or if you actually have a lot in common with Mike and really like him. I know you're probably not thinking of marriage and I don't necessarily expect you to marry the first boy you sleep with. But I still believe that if you're not to hurt yourself, the fullness of the relationship is important. I'd like you to think about this and we can talk about it further if you want. And Debbie, don't forget that if you have any problems you can share them with me.

DEBBIE: Thanks, Mom.

Debbie is probably relieved that she has been found out and that she has a responsible adult to confide in, at least partially. Her mother has not reacted in an exaggerated fashion, but tactfully, and she can now be trusted by her daughter to behave sensibly. The basis for a continuing dialogue has been set up.

Misinformation and Exaggeration

Much familial tension is due to the parents' misinformation and subsequent exaggeration of the hazards of such aspects of the adolescent culture as drug-taking. It is crucial that parents, if they are to maintain their children's respect and trust, not involve themselves in rash statements that can only engender a credibility gap. Adolescents do not forgive easily, nor do they forget that their parents have made a mistake on one point and hence are liable to be mistaken in other areas. The father who, as in our profile of Mr. Henderson, exaggerates the danger of drugs, causes his child to escalate the situation by defending all drugs, even though the teenager may know very well that not all drugs are safe. However, exaggeration evokes an over-reaction; and a tyrannical attitude based on misinformation can only alienate the adolescent totally from his parents.

The parent who insists that marijuana-smoking will lead to heroin addiction or to involvement in the criminal underworld, or who makes unreasoned statements about the terrors of drugs and the physical decay which follows on the heels of a "pep pill," is jeopardizing his credibility vis-à-vis the teenager. If a parent is totally convinced of the undesirability of adolescent drug use, and wishes to avoid it, then he can adapt the following model to the particular situation at hand.

FATHER: David, I've been reading that more and more kids of high school age are taking drugs, and it worries me. I don't want you to get involved in that and if you've already experimented with some drugs, I'd like you to stop.

SON: But why, Dad? Most of the drugs aren't harmful and I pretty well know what is and what isn't dangerous.

FATHER: Well, son. I've been doing some of my own research into this question and from what I can see, all drugs are dangerous to some extent. Besides, there really hasn't been any conclusive

150

evidence on the safety of drugs.

SON: That isn't fair, Dad. I think I'm old enough to decide on my own what can harm me and what can't. I don't tell you to stop drinking.

FATHER: First of all, I drink very little — and I know what I'm getting in my shot of whiskey. But let's not get sidetracked. It's not only the potential physical danger of drugs which worries me, but the way in which it can affect your school work and your whole outlook on life. I don't want to be tyrannical and forbid you to smoke the occasional marijuana cigarette. But I do feel that the less you have to do with the drug scene the better. There's enough of interest in the world that we can perceive and experience with our senses just as they are to make drug use quite unnecessary. Furthermore, it's extremely important in this complex age of ours to maintain our reasoning powers intact. You're not going to solve any of your own or the world's problems by escaping into a pleasurable cloud of marijuana. Do you see what I mean, Dave?

SON: Yeah, Dad, I see your point. But I can't promise never to smoke marijuana again.

FATHER: I don't expect you to make any promises you can't keep, Dave. But do keep in mind what I've said. And don't let your friends influence you too much. They're not always right about everything, you know.

The father here has explained his stand in a reasonable way, and even if his son does not fully follow his advice, one can imagine that he will keep his father's argument in mind. Furthermore, by not exaggerating the dangers of drugs, and by not reacting hysterically to his son's toned-down espousal of drug use, the father has managed to keep his son within the bounds of productive dialogue, rather than to estrange him. It is never fruitful in a family situation to make arbitrary judgments, based either on self-righteousness or on a lack of information. Parents as well as adolescents must recognize that on most issues there is no *one* just stand. Such matters as drug use, inter-racial relationships, war, and politics can be argued intelligently from many sides. Neither parents nor teenagers can state emphatically that only their view is right — as if it were a direct message from some all-knowing divinity. These views are matters of opinion, not of indisputable law. The father who says to his son, "You're going to end up in the gutter — all drug-users do," will only cause his son to rebel dramatically against his proclamations. First of all, the information is wrong, and the youngster is aware of this. Secondly, his person is being judged and attacked, rather than the situation at hand. An arbitrary evaluation of character such as this is totally unhelpful and may provoke the adolescent either to live out his father's prediction or to immerse himself in the drug culture precisely to prove to his father that he can withstand it.

There is another type of exaggeration related to drugs that parents resort to, and this is the reverse of the scare tactic. Rather than alienate their children, some parents feel that they must keep up with them, and they behave in an exaggerated fashion by trying to partake of their children's drug culture and drug experience. Hence they turn on, perhaps with their children, perhaps only in order to discuss the sensation with them. Our experience with the adolescent children of such parents shows that most often teenagers resent the intrusion of their parents into what they see as their own domain. Usually, they consider it undignified on the parent's part, and would prefer that parents maintain a degree of distance. Most of the adolescents we have known have indicated considerable discomfort with, and contempt for, adults who try to become part of the youth culture. They do not admire parent drug users, imitation of hip talk, or emulation of adolescent dress and customs. In some instances, an adolescent will taunt his parents with: "What do you know? You haven't even tried any drugs." An occasional parent will fall into this trap and try so as to be able to "communicate on the adolescent's level." The point, however, is not whether the parent has a pleasurable experience, because this completely overlooks the various hazards and liabilities of drug use as already described, but rather that the adolescent is likely to feel contemptuous of the parent who does not act like an adult. Inconsistent as this may seem, it remains part of the adolescent's make-up.

Escalation of Minor Difficulties

In many contemporary households, minor points of contention between parent and adolescent are blown up to such proportions that a virtual termination of communication results. This is extremely dangerous, since the accrued tension makes it impossible for the child to call upon the parent or to trust him should a serious difficulty occur. It is essential that parents, by their behavior and expression, make their children feel that in times of stress, they can always be counted upon to give a helping hand, without imposing on the child a burden of guilt for the emotional, financial, or legal support offered.

Minor difficulties can usually be relieved by a compromise. The intransigent parent breeds an intransigent child. But if any kind of dialogue is to be maintained in the family, it is necessary for both parents and adolescents to discuss what they consider reasonable obligations, limits, and needs. In most families, there is some argument as to time put in doing homework, restrictions on dating hours and dating possibilities, school attendance, use of the car, tasks to be performed about the house, and so on. If these day-to-day occurrences cannot be agreed upon with a relative degree of mutual satisfaction, then it will be impossible for the family to discuss what are certainly the more important matters of drug-use, sex, the possibility of dropping out of school or career choice, and perhaps inter-racial dating.

Some form of satisfactory compromise can be arrived at for all minor points of contention. It is just as unreasonable for a parent to expect a teenager to spend all his free time doing school work as it is for the teenager to stay out every evening until the early hours of the morning. The family beset by such problems should call a meeting for all the parties involved so that some form of agreement can be reached. Both parents and adolescents will be surprised at how easily a modus vivendi can be arrived at when neither side is beset by hostility and both are willing to be reasonable. Here is a possible dialogue.

FATHER: Jean, I know we've been arguing lately about all kinds of things. But your mother and I think it's time that we sat down and talked it all out calmly, so that we can have some peace in the family. This constant haggling makes none of us very happy.

DAUGHTER: O.K., Dad. I'm tired of it all too. But if we're going to talk, that doesn't mean that I'm to be lectured at.

FATHER: Right you are, Jean. I know I have a tendency to lecture at you — but I'll try not to. It's just that I feel very strongly about some things.

DAUGHTER: I understand, Dad. And I'll try not to get angry.

MOTHER: The first thing I think we should discuss is dating hours. You've been staying out quite late almost every night. It's not the idea of staying out late that bothers me, it's just that I can't see how you can get all your homework done. And you look very tired in the mornings. You're quite pale lately.

FATHER: Your mother's right about that, Jean. Can you think of some reasonable compromise?

DAUGHTER: How would it be if I stay out on weekends and only one night during the week, like Wednesdays? I don't mind not going out all the time, if you don't scream at me all the time that I'm here. That's one of the reasons I'm always out. But besides that, I do think it's unfair for me to have to clean up Steve's room and mine, plus do the supper dishes. He's old enough to help around the house and it would give me more time for my homework. How about it? I do the dishes three times a week and my room every day.

FATHER: Fine, Jean. Now if you don't break your side of the agreement, we won't hassle you. Is that clear?

MOTHER: That sounds quite good.

Minor problems having been cleared up, the family can discuss other issues with some degree of understanding on both sides. It is important in such situations of compromise to allow the youngster to determine what are suitable limits and thereby concretize his own desire for autonomy. If Jean in our dialogue states the terms of the bargain herself, suggests that she go out three nights of the week and stay home the rest of the time, then she is far more likely to keep to the agreement than if these terms are imposed on her. She is satisfying her desire for independence, and her parents are allowing her to prove that she can act and reason like a mature being.

One of the most tension-promoting questions in the contemporary home is that of inter-racial and inter-religious dating. Parents tend to flare up irrationally at the thought of their teenager going out with someone of another race or religion. They seem always to think that, especially in the case of a daughter, marriage or perhaps pregnancy is imminent, and they lay down intransigent laws which seem unfair and ridiculous to the young. The young rebel against such tyrannical behavior, sometimes with great harm to themselves. In such cases it is really up to the adolescent to take the lead and try to explain to his parents why he finds their point of view alien to him and his generation's way of life.

Parents' stands on the issue of inter-racial dating can often not be changed, but it is important that they make their reasons for this clear to the adolescent; and if they cannot change how they feel, at least they can point out to him that even though they disagree radically on this one point, the entire family relationship need not be jeopardized because of this. Even parents who profess liberal views often find it difficult to see their own child dating someone of a different race. The adolescent should try to understand that this is due to the older generation's upbringing and to fears for their children's future happiness. Whatever the case, the parent should not impose a tyrannical set of rules which may make the child feel that he is an outcast in his own home if he does not abide by them, or that he has nowhere to turn in a moment of crisis. In addition, parents who impose tyrannical and arbitrary rules only run the risk that their children will continue relationships behind their parents' backs. If an adolescent is determined to see someone, there is really nothing that the parent can do to legislate the relationship out of existence. Parental determination to forbid frequently leads to adolescent determination to continue to do what has been forbidden. In any event, the door to further communication and a possible change of mind should never be closed.

Let us continue the dialogue between Jean and her parents and imagine them discussing the question of inter-racial dating.

JEAN: All right. Once we're all talking calmly, I want to get the main point into the open. As you know, I've been seeing a lot of Joel and I think that's the main reason you've been hassling me so much.

MOTHER: You're right. It really bothers us, and though we don't want to forbid it, we still think that you would be better off dating a white boy. I'm sure that there are a lot of nice white boys around.

FATHER: Your mother's right, Jean! I don't see why you can't go out with a white boy. I'm sure you'd have a lot more in common. And besides, you're getting near marriageable age and I would really put my foot down at that. You don't know how much trouble you'd have in life being married to a black.

DAUGHTER: Oh Dad, that's absolutely ridiculous. We're not going to live in Mississippi. Besides, that's not the point. I don't intend to get married for a long time yet, if ever. What really makes you nervous is that your friends will see me out with Joel, and say, "Oh, just look at that Cross girl. Isn't that shameful." Well, that really doesn't bother me in the least. It's time you people got rid of your prejudices.

MOTHER: I agree, Jean. We wouldn't like our friends to know about it. But believe me, that's not the main point. Have you ever thought seriously of the consequences of a mixed marriage?

DAUGHTER: But Mom, I told you. I'm not about to get married to Joel. We're friends. Now look, try to understand this. When you went to school, everyone in your school was white, or at least ninety percent were — right? You don't even know what blacks are like. Things have changed now. Half or more of the kids in school are black. We all study together, go out together . . . You, who pretend to believe in equality and all that . . . I don't know how you can act this way. I'll tell you what — I'll bring Joel over for dinner one night and you can see for yourselves what a great guy he is.

FATHER: Well, I don't know about that. Things might be a little uncomfortable.

DAUGHTER: Oh come on, Dad. Be adventurous. The world is changing, you know.

FATHER: All right. But this doesn't alter anything I said earlier. I still don't want you marrying a black.

DAUGHTER: O.K., O.K., we'll worry about that if we ever come to it, and you just might surprise yourselves and actually enjoy Joel.

Even though many troubled parents may not be able to achieve the degree of control and willingness to cooperate which is visible in this dialogue, it is still something to be aimed at. To be intransigent about questions of inter-racial dating or drug use is, these days, to appear fossilized to the young. Furthermore, intransigence may induce the teenager to rebel violently against his parents and drive him precisely into the situation his parents have forbidden him to even imagine. The only validity of that situation may be that it is in direct opposition to his parents' stipulations; and once he is removed from familial pressure he may realize that it was a false one and harmful to him. Once again, a compromise or a modicum of understanding must be aimed at, if parents and adolescents do not want to live in a constant and wearing atmosphere of hostility.

The Perfect Child Syndrome

There are three different forms of the "perfect child syndrome" and each of these constitutes a parental attitude which can be harmful to the teenager and even bring on disastrous consequences. In the first case, we have the parent who *demands* perfection from his child. No matter what the youngster does, no matter how good his grades are, or how great his achievement in non-academic fields, he fails to live up to his parent's ideal youth. More children than one would imagine bring home fully satisfactory report cards only to be told, "That's not bad, Johnny, but you can do much better. Why, when I was your age . . . " This kind of attitude can force the youth into a vicious struggle for his parents' approval. Frustration is intense, for it is unlikely that he will ever match his parent's ideal of perfection. The youngster who recognizes the impossibility of becoming the person of his parent's dreams may just give up the struggle totally and succumb to never being good enough. He can lose all sense of his own self-esteem, believe that he will always be an incompetent, and thus be seriously hampered in later life.

Parents should never expect perfection from their children and they should especially refrain from verbalizing such an attitude. Every person wishes to be recognized and approved of for what he is and has done and not be measured against some absent and invisible standard. In our work with adolescents, we have found that it is exceedingly important to manifest approval for what the young have accomplished, rather than to stress where they have failed. The teenager is usually sufficiently self-conscious and self-critical. He needs to be reinforced rather than derided if the parents wish him to mature into a person capable of coping with the demands of the adult world.

We are not saying that there is no situation in which the parent cannot encourage the child to do better or even do more things, but this must follow upon a realistic appraisal of the youngster's possibilities. If Johnnie is bad at sports, but an avid reader, it is more important that he be praised for what he has accomplished than denigrated for something for which he has no taste or ability. On the other hand, if a parent feels that a youngster can do better, and is not living up to his potential because of laziness or subsidiary interests, the parent can, in a tactful way, point this out. There may be something bothering the youngster that the parent has not noticed, and this may be a good way of exploring the problem.

MOTHER: Johnny, you haven't been doing all that well in school lately. Your teachers tell me it's not because you're not capable; they all think you're very bright, but they say you've been skipping classes and not preparing for class. Is something wrong?

SON: Oh Mom, there's nothing wrong. I just find school boring. All the subjects are dull or irrelevant. There's no point my working at these things. Besides, I'm doing well enough.

MOTHER: Not really, Johnny. You'll never get into a good college if you go on this way. And I've always thought that that is what you wanted.

SON: There is plenty of time to worry about college, yet, Mom.

MOTHER: No there isn't Johnny. You must see that. It's not all that far away. I can understand that you might find some of your school subjects dull, but they still have to be done. And it's up to you to make things more interesting for yourself. If Dad and I can help in any way, if you'd like to review what you're studying about in any particular subject at dinner, we'd be only too happy to listen.

SON: Well, maybe. But there are other things I have to think about now.

MOTHER: Want to tell me about them?

SON: Not right now, Mom. Maybe in a little while. I'm pretty depressed.

MOTHER: I can understand that Johnny. Things don't always go as we wish them to, but your father and I want you to work a little harder. In any case, absolutely no skipping classes. We don't want you to regret this later on.

SON: All right, Mom. I'll try.

Johnny's mother is not identifying his failure in school with an inherent part of his character. She is not judging or evaluating him, but focusing her attention on the problem at hand. Furthermore, while never giving up her main argument in favor of school, she is trying to relate to Johnny's feelings, to recognize them and acknowledge them, thereby showing her youngster that she can understand how he feels. So often, parents refuse to see that their children may be feeling something, experiencing an emotion, which is at the basis of their negative activity. Johnny may be failing in school because he is depressed over interpersonal difficulties, or his apparently unglamorous life, or whatever. The fact that his mother can empathize with his depression may ease it for him, and will certainly improve the possibility of communication.

Another behavioral possibility within the perfect child syndrome is the parent who casually expects perfection from the child and hence, is never surprised or overly pleased by what the child achieves. This is the kind of parent who, no matter how well the child performs, merely says, "Of course you did well. You're my son aren't you?" It is accepted that the child will be outstanding in whatever he undertakes to do. Thus the youngster is never sufficiently reinforced for his achievement. He may, in reaction, begin to think that it is hardly worth the effort of doing well, and allow himself to slide downhill. More dramatically, he may feel that the only way to induce a reaction from his parents is to do something unspeakably destructive, thereby forcing his parents to pay attention to him because of their surprise.

An extension and variation of this parental attitude is the parent who deludes himself into believing his child is perfect. Thus, he denies the possibility of the child ever doing any wrong, and refuses to see that the youngster may be encountering psychological, social, or academic difficulties. Such parents, even if they are told that their youngster seems to be failing in school, obstinately refuse to see this as a real threat to their vision of the child's perfection. They will make the excuse that this failure is temporary, due either to a teacher's mismanagement or an incomprehensible dislike of the child. They constantly evade the reality of a situation.

The child of such parents has a double burden to bear. He lives under the constant threat of being found out, for he himself realizes that in no way does he compare to his parent's image of him. He fears their love is only directed at this false image, not at his real being. Furthermore, he must always try to live up to this image, so that the chances of being "found out" are lessened. His adolescent struggle to find his true identity is made extremely difficult, since he already has two distinct persons to cope with: his parent's illusory image of him and what he sees as his far less perfect self.

The sensitive youngster may lead himself into serious trouble, given such parents. On the one hand, he may try to force his parents into recognizing what he considers his real person by blatantly committing grave misdeeds, and hoping that by this tactic his parents will, at some point, realize that he is not this perfect youth, but an adolescent with problems which need to be discussed and shared. On the other hand, the youngster's problems may be aggravated and increased by the fact that he must constantly hide them from his parents since he feels the shock of discovery will lead to his complete rejection. The danger of the parent's constant denial can be seen in the fact that we have in our records three cases of suicide brought about by precisely this kind of parental denial of the very real problems of their child. Pseudo-suicides, however, are far more frequent and the parents who neglect to see that a youngster is acting out his needs, is crying for help by involving himself in self-destructive activities, may suddenly find themselves in grave straits.

Calls for help, or pseudo-suicides, can take various forms. The youngster who has normally done well in school may quite suddenly start doing badly, skipping classes, or playing truant altogether. He may become a heavy drug user. He may, having been a fairly gregarious person, suddenly isolate himself from all external forms of contact.

The wise parent cannot deny the importance of such sudden shifts and disregard them as mere "phases" in an otherwise "perfect" life. They may be "phases," but it is much more likely that they constitute a plea for attention, for help, and for recognition of the youngster's problems and needs. In either case, it is essential that the parent make a realistic evaluation of the situation and not deny the possibility of the youngster having real problems. To do otherwise is sheer escapism and a refusal to face the responsibilities of parenthood.

Let us see how a parent who has always believed that his youngster is a near-perfect child, but has recently had it forced upon his attention that a problem does exist, could react. The situation must be handled delicately, if the parent is not to alienate the child further.

MOTHER: Sandy, your guidance counsellor phoned me from school today. She tells me you haven't been in school for the past two

160

weeks. Please tell me if it's true. Is there something wrong? Aren't you feeling well?

SANDY: Oh I'm feeling all right, Mom. I'm just fed up with school. I'm going to drop out.

MOTHER: Sandy, you can't do that. Why that would mean . . . Listen, there must be something troubling you. You're not being yourself.

SANDY: I am, Mom. You just don't know me at all. You've never wanted to know me.

MOTHER: I'm sorry I've given you that impression. It's not true, you know. I want to know you very much and all about you. Please tell me what's wrong. Perhaps your father and I can help.

SANDY: *(silence)*

MOTHER: Sandy, we love you, no matter what you do. Now please tell me. Don't be afraid to speak out. I want to know whatever it is. I promise I won't get hysterical.

SANDY: I don't know why you're suddenly concerned. After all, I'm the perfect girl, aren't I? There couldn't be anything wrong with me. I couldn't possibly have any serious problems. . . . Well, could I?

MOTHER: I guess you do, if you're seriously considering dropping out of school. Look, let's try and forget how your father and I have acted toward you in the past. I know it's difficult for you, but I'm willing to admit that perhaps we haven't been ideal parents. I'm really worried about you now, Sandy, and I want to help. Do tell me why you want to drop out.

SANDY: Oh Mom, I just can't face it any more. This constant drudgery. I'd like a change of scene, to go away for a long while.

MOTHER: I really don't think that's wise, not as a permanent decision. Look, there are only a few weeks left until Christmas, and if you really feel troubled, perhaps I could arrange for both of us to go away for a while, or perhaps you'd rather be alone and have time to think, then you could start fresh after Christmas. We could get permission from your teachers, see what has to be done until then, and work on it together. I'm sure you don't want to lose a whole year of school.

SANDY: Well, maybe, Mom. I really feel awful. I've gotten mixed up with this group of kids . . . and I really don't like them and don't want to see them. I don't know how I'll be able to come back after Christmas.

MOTHER: You can't run away from things. Maybe that's what I've been doing, and it makes things worse. Perhaps after you've had a little rest and change, things will look a little different.

We are not offering this as a total solution to Sandy's problem, but at least her mother has made it known to her that she is willing to recognize her problems as real, share them, and if possible help her out. This may work. But if Sandy's problems are more deeply rooted and she is agreeable to getting help from the outside, then a family visit to a social worker or psychologist may be called for. It should, however, be a family visit, at least at first, so that the youngster is not once again thrust totally on her own resources and made to feel that her parents are denying her problems.

Adolescents, too, are sometimes guilty of inflicting the "perfection syndrome" on their parents. This consists of the child constantly accusing the parent of not living up to his expectations of parenthood. Adolescents should, however, be mature enough to realize that there is no such thing as the perfect parent, just as there is no perfect child. The parent is consistently faced by problems outside the home and this may make him irritable with the youngster or disinclined to pay attention to him, when this attention is demanded. Sensitivity to the other person's state of mind is always necessary. There is no need to take every comment excessively to heart and interpret it as a sign of disapproval.

Sharing and Its Limits

Throughout this chapter we have stressed that it is essential for adolescents and their parents to share problems, experiences, and ideas, so that they can come to a better understanding of each other. If the family is to be a unit wherein each individual is at ease and trusts the other, that is necessary. However, there are limits to this sharing, a subtle demarcation line that each family must determine for itself so that relations do not become psychologically incestuous or overburdening. There are many aspects of individual adult life which it is better for the parent not to inflict on his children and, conversely, aspects of adolescent's life which the parent should not press the youngster to recount. A respect for privacy is as important to family harmony as is the feeling that in moments of crisis the youngster can depend on his elders.

Let us look at some concrete configurations of this problem. While it is important for adolescents to know something of their parents' life outside the home as well as something of their past life, it is unwise for parents to share marital difficulties with the youngster. This only forces the adolescent to take sides in parental quarrels and inflicts a burden upon him with which he does not want to, and often cannot, cope. It makes the youngster uncomfortable to be confronted with the intricacies of his parents' relationships. We realize that within the small circle of the family, it may sometimes be impossible for parents to restrain antagonistic feelings toward one another in front of their children. But to oversee a quarrel is somehow not as disturbing to the youngster as to be forced to participate, to take sides, or to become a confederate.

The father or mother who forces the adolescent to play an active role in marital disputes is being highly destructive toward the adolescent.

There is another kind of enforced sharing which is common in some families and is equally disturbing to the youngster. We have all heard or read of the mother who waits up until all hours of the night for her daughter to come in so that she can question her about her whereabouts and experiences. Again, there is nothing wrong with a limited degree of sharing, but the adolescent will quite naturally resent an intrusion into areas which she considers wholly personal. There is an element of vicarious living in this kind of insistence on the revelation of all aspects of the child's experience, and the adolescent, who is attempting to consolidate her own separate identity, is likely to react with hostility to such a situation. The daughter may be quite willing to tell the mother where she has been and with whom, but to be asked to describe aspects of her sexual encounters is an infringement on her privacy.

Frequently, parents who insist on total sharing force their children into a defensive and stubborn silence concerning even the minutest aspects of their lives outside the home. They resent what they may sense is their parents' attempt to live their lives over through them, or what they interpret as a tactic to keep them dependent on their parents. The parent who wishes to maintain a close relationship with his child must intuit how much the youngster is prepared to reveal willingly, and refrain from forcing him to speak of things he prefers to keep private. Again, tact and respect for individual privacy are necessary.

If the adolescent feels that his parents are overly and unjustly inquisitive, it is up to him to explain in a reasonable fashion just how much he is willing to share and how much he wishes to keep to himself. Here is a possible way of confronting the situation. A daughter has just come in from a late date and her mother is waiting up for her.

MOTHER: Tina, I can hardly keep my eyes open, it's so late. Where have you been?

DAUGHTER: Oh, I went to the movies and then to a party with Robert.

MOTHER: What film did you see? Was it good?

DAUGHTER: Not bad. We went to see *Joe*. It's about a girl who is on drugs and her father, a straight executive, murders her boyfriend and finally ends up by shooting her as well as all her friends. Stupid man, really. He's got a truck driver friend called Joe, who's completely out of his mind . . . in an American way.

MOTHER: Oh yes. I read about that. That's the film about the hippies, isn't it?

DAUGHTER: It's supposed to be about hippies. But it's really a very slanted portrayal of them, one-sided. All they show them doing is taking drugs and making love. It's not that simple. You should go see it though, then you'll know what I'm talking about.

MOTHER: I will. What happened at the party you went to?

DAUGHTER: Oh, we all sat around and rapped. Danced a bit too.

MOTHER: Is that all? Really?

DAUGHTER: More or less. If there's any more, I'm not really prepared to talk about it now. There are some things I like to keep to myself.

MOTHER: I don't want you to hide anything from me, Tina.

DAUGHTER: Oh, I'm not hiding anything Mom. But there are some things I just prefer not to talk about. They're my business. I'm not going to go around telling you how I kissed Robert . . . that's ridiculous. And it's my business.

MOTHER: All right, dear. I can understand that, I guess. But if you ever want to tell me anything, you know I'm willing to listen. Good-night.

The daughter, here, has shared certain aspects of her evening with her mother and carefully pointed out that there are other things which she prefers to keep private. Her mother wisely respects her privacy, but also suggests that she is always willing to hear what her daughter may have to tell her, thereby leaving the road open to future communication. It is important for parents to have this regard for the more personal aspects of their youngsters' lives if they wish to maintain the possibility of interchange in the family and allow their children to develop into responsible and independent adults.

The Smother

There are many parents who find it exceedingly difficult to allow their children to grow up and hence away from them. Since adolescence is essentially a period in which the youngster must test his powers outside the family circle and prove his independence, an over-protective parent may instigate serious conflict and even damage the youngster's ability to develop into a mature adult. The ability to let go of the youngster at an appropriate period in his development is perhaps one of the most crucial duties the parents must learn to fulfill. To hold on to the youngster, to refuse to treat him as a young adult rather than an overgrown child, can have negative consequences. The smothering parents who insist that they must protect their youngster from the shocks of existence, who deny him the possibility of self-sufficient responsible action, and who overwhelm him with care, may find themselves confronted with a hostile rebel who resents and reacts against their every move, or with a life-long dependent.

Adolescence is a time when the youngster must break away from parental control and must experiment with life . . . even though this experimentation may appear negative to his parents, and often constitute some degree of rebellion. There are many instances in the adolescent experience when the youngster must act for himself, and while hopefully the parent can communicate with him, he cannot act for him or make decisions for him. It is ultimately up to the adolescent to decide for himself what his position is on drugs, sex, schooling, and career. If his parents have inculcated values in him which stress human integrity and the importance of intellectual and emotional growth, they should trust him to make positive decisions.

Parental limits can of course be set, attitudes clarified; but arbitrary demands or unqualified orders will only force the youngster to transgress against parental policy.

There are several characteristics of "smothering" which the parent can detect in himself if he wishes to make an honest appraisal of his situation: endless interrogation of a non-responsive youngster suggests that the parent is overstepping the bounds of privacy and fledgling independence. An overwhelming desire to possess all aspects of the youngster's experience, to demand intimate knowledge of his activities outside the home and to be present at all his activities within the home, is a second characteristic. Unwillingness to trust the youngster's competence, to permit him to spend any extended period of time away from home, and a need to perform a variety of tasks for him which he could just as easily do for himself is another. All these attitudes intimate an overprotectiveness on the parents' part.

Mothers who no longer have young children to care for and have geared their lives to bringing up their young often have some difficulty in this area. They wish to keep their teenagers as children, partially in an attempt to maintain their own youth and partially because the vacuity of a life in which one's primary role is no longer of use can be hard to face. Thus they baby their adolescents, try to live their lives for them, or experience their lives vicariously. This can be harmful to both parties. Sharing, as we have mentioned, should have its limits. Teenagers have told us that they would be happy to share things with such overprotective mothers if only these things could be shared on an adult level, where each side acknowledges the validity of the other's opinions and feelings. Some of these teenagers have suggested that their mothers enroll in university courses, or engage in community activity or political work, so that certain experiences could be common to both and shared in a mature way. Such parents often feel envious of other adults who seem to have captured their youngsters' respect and intimacy. If they manifest a sufficient distance from their young and a willingness to respect their children's independence, they could play a similar role in their teenagers' lives.

Let us look at a typical situation involving an over-protective mother. The youngster wishes to go to the country with some friends for the weekend and the mother is frightened and unwilling to permit this. It is up to the teenager here to prove his competence and responsibility and for the mother to recognize the reality of this and the importance of "letting go."

SON: Mom, Tim has invited George and me up to his country house for the weekend. It's in a beautiful spot near a lake in New Hampshire. May I go?

MOTHER: No, No, Paul, absolutely not. I'd be worried sick about you, wondering every minute whether you were all right, whether the car had broken down, whether you had drowned . . . God knows what.

SON: Mom, that's ridiculous. I'm not a child anymore. You can't keep your eye on me every minute. If you keep on this way, soon you'll be taking me by the hand and walking me to school.

MOTHER: It's not the same thing, Paul. I know what you're doing when you're at school and I don't worry.

SON: You don't know. You just believe that, so it's all right. You trust me that far and no further. What will you do when I'm away at college?

MOTHER: I try not to think about it, it's too upsetting.

SON: Look Mom, sooner or later you're going to have to face the fact that I'm growing up. You can't build your life around me anymore. Anyhow I'm quite capable of managing for myself. Have I ever had a bad car accident? No. Have I ever drowned? No. Did you ever have to bail me out of jail? No. Well . . . You're going to have to grow up too.

MOTHER: But I can't help worrying about you.

SON: Well, that just makes me miserable. Do I have to imagine you at home worrying, every time I make a move outside the house. Come on, Mom, I'm old enough to be trusted, and I do want to go to the country. I haven't been anywhere for months and it will be a nice change.

MOTHER: All right, I give in, but promise you'll phone me as soon as you get there and before you leave.

SON: O.K. This time I will, but you can't expect that forever. You'll have to find other things to think about besides me.

If the youngster can and has in the past proved his competence and dependability, there is no call for over-protectiveness. Parents must recognize that adolescents are not possessions whose surroundings can always be ordered and controlled. There is a time when

167

freedom from parents is necessary. We have known many young-sters whose mothers could not bring themselves to "let go;" the consequences have all too often been a teenager who does exactly as he pleases while lying about what he is doing.

The dialogues in this chapter do not provide ultimate solutions to tense family situations. We have merely tried to concretize those attitudes and remarks that may cause friction in the family, and attempted to show possible ways of neutralizing these by certain modes of communication. There can be no positive assurance that adolescents or adults will immediately respond favorably to the tac-tics we have sketched. The road to trust and harmonious family existence can be slow and sometimes painful. However, if both youngsters and parents recognize aspects of their own behavior in this chapter and attempt to refrain from constantly repeating and engaging in what we have described as negative forms of expression and action, then trust and contact can slowly be established. Honesty, explanation, evaluation, and a willingness to recognize the fact that there is always more than one valid point of view for each problem, are necessary at *all* times and in *all* situations. The parent who simply puts his foot down and says "I won't have it" runs a grave risk of losing all meaningful contact with his youngster. Moreover, since there is no way to "police" an adolescent's activi-ties, the parent is unlikely to have his way in any event. The teen-ager who insists on having his way, regardless of his parents' feelings, runs the risk of creating a situation of open warfare. Both sides must recognize that without the capacity for compromise, individuals can exist, but they cannot function as a family unit.

168

IN SUMMING UP

What can be done to ease tension between the generations? The intricate stresses and strains of family life have long
posed a problem to psychologists, and in our rapidly changing,
relatively unstructured culture, no ideal model of the family exists.
One can only suggest and reemphasize that, if understanding
between parent and adolescent is to be attained, a dialogue based
on trust, mutual respect, and a sharing of individual experience
must be established in the family. This is no easy task. It involves
a willingness on the parents' part to recognize the teenager as a
young adult who must experience life independently, form his own
world view, and necessarily grow away from the family. If this
growing up and away includes a critique of parental values, or a
rebellion against the parents' life style, parents must have the personal strength to consider the validity of this critique as well as to
make an effort to recognize this rebellion as a necessary period of
experimentation in the adolescent's life. To be able to let go of the
youngster, to allow him to form his own identity, is an essential
feature of parenthood.

This does not mean that parents should allow themselves to be

169

harassed by, or to give financial support to, a youngster who is abusing drugs and generally "copping out," for this amounts to babying and is another way of stifling possible maturity. Clear limits can be set, so that the youngster has some sense of structured values, but parental limits should involve an understanding of the youth culture. For example, if the teenager feels that college has no relevance to him and insists on dropping out, then other forms of meaningful activity can be discussed: VISTA, the Peace Corps, community work such as tutoring children in street schools. Not everyone must be confined to the sphere of academic development. The adolescent can have a positive experience out of school through which he can test his own worth and begin to feel that he has an ability to make some small mark on the world. Though parents can set up guidelines for other kinds of meaningful activities, it is important that specific suggestions *come from the adolescent,* so that he can live up to his own expectations. On the other hand, there is no need for parents to be shamed or bullied into supporting a youngster who may just be indulging his sensations while mouthing radical slogans or professing profound inner development. In all cases there is a necessity for understanding followed by clearheaded evaluation.

Adolescents, too, have a responsibility and a major role to play in the easing of household tension. They must measure to what extent their criticism of their parents or their choice of a life style is a pure reaction or rebellion against their elders' way of life and to what extent it is a true expression of their beliefs. There is little point in chanting to one's parents something akin to one of Bob Dylan's refrains: "You don't know what you're doing, do you Mr. Jones?," for this merely serves to build an infrangible mystique around the superiority of youth culture which necessarily alienates and angers parents. Wholesale judgments of this kind create hostility where there is a need for understanding. So do such shouted slogans as "You're just a Fascist pig!" Every parent has a life experience of some kind which deserves to be understood. The young who place such value on experience and its immediacy, may find, if they draw their parents out, that there is in each adult life some set of observations and experiences which is interesting in itself, which makes the turn the parents' life may have taken comprehensible, and which paves the way to mutual understanding. Furthermore, if the teenager wishes to be treated as an independent individual, he has the obligation of explaining his views to his parents and of acting responsibly so that he gains the trust of his elders.

Both generations must face the double burden of honesty, even if this means momentary unpleasantness. Parents should not be afraid to express their mixed feelings and fears about drugs, interracial dating, sexual permissiveness, or whatever the case may be. It is better for teenagers to know exactly where parents stand on such controversial issues, than for them to be confronted by unexpected hysteria or over-reaction after what seemed a permitted act has been committed. Inversely, adolescents must see that their parents' fears about various aspects of the drug culture are often valid despite what the adolescent may feel at the moment. These misgivings are frequently grounded in a firm appreciation of reality.

Honesty toward one another is complemented by honesty with oneself. This entails the ability to face criticism openly, to say that perhaps one's views are not total and can be modified, to acknowledge that one's way of life is not the only possible one, and that valid alternatives exist. This particular form of honesty is perhaps the most difficult for both parents and adolescents.

However one looks at it, there is no future to being young. Parents who attempt to shelter their youngsters from experience and thus forestall any possible maturity ought to take note of this inevitable fact. So too might youngsters who ardently attest to the value of the youth culture and instinctively shut their ears to whatever may be said by someone who has outgrown "youth." One may be "out of date" when one reaches the climactic age of twenty-five, but life continues.

This does not mean that the critical mirror youth holds up to age may not in many ways be valid. Nor does it mean that when the NOW generation matures, it will replicate the parental generation, even though the responsibilities of maturity may pose some problems youth does not now foresee. What is needed on the level of personal and family relations is renewed focus on common elements, on shared needs and experiences, rather than on discrepancies in fashion or differences in outlook. Long or short hair, jeans or crinolines, marijuana or alcohol — the amount of domestic irritation that has accumulated around these superficialities of life certainly surpasses their actual importance. A more significant differentiation between the generations is the emphasis among youth upon an inward focus rather than a life directed toward external success, and the development of a social conscience that overrides desires for personal gain. One must not minimize the importance of this new orientation in American youth, for its social and political implications are great.

On the other hand, it is necessary for both generations to see — if only within the family — that these differences are differences in expression of human needs common to all. We all — black, white, young, old — desire to love and to be loved. We all search for fulfillment, though some may find it in an inward orientation and others in attaining external success. We all wish to be accepted, admired, respected by our fellows, however we seek out and identify these "fellows." This may ring of humanist platitudes, but it is nevertheless an undisputed fact. If within the family parents and teenagers can recognize these human similarities, then enmity can develop into understanding and tolerance of differences.

More practically, what is a parent or an adolescent to do when he feels that family tension has reached a point beyond endurance? Often it is a good idea for the teenager to stay with relatives or friends for a week or so until tensions subside. Often teenagers can explain their case more clearly to other adults than to their parents. A friend or another adult who has a relationship with the conflicting family members could be asked to mediate.

On a community basis, parent and adolescent groups can be organized in an attempt to set up a generational dialogue. This might involve several groups of half a dozen parents and half a dozen teenagers, not the children of those particular parents, holding weekly "rap" sessions in which family problems and generational differences of outlook can be discussed. The problems which occur in various families tend to be remarkably similar and both generations are quicker to come to an understanding when they are not threatened by the presence of their own family members. The ultimate outcome of these weekly sessions would be to have family members participate in the same group to see what has been learned.

In a situation of extreme tension, it is in no way humiliating to ask for professional help. The youngster can go to a social worker or psychological counsellor individually, but it is sometimes more helpful for all members of the family to participate in family therapy. This permits the professional to see all sides of the picture and to point out to those concerned exactly where the relationships, the connecting links between the members of the family rather than the individuals themselves, may be going wrong.

Adolescence, as we have said time and time again, is a period of life fraught with difficulties and tensions, both for the adolescent and the parent. The manifold possibilities, injustices, and disappointments of existence are revealed to the youngster for the first time, and he may find himself overwhelmed, unable to cope, and tormented by his relative ineffectuality. He may only dimly or unconsciously perceive his restlessness and rebellion. Minor matters may become the focus of a major conflict and he is liable to fall prey to influences that do not serve him well. It is up to parents at such a juncture to provide at least some form of leadership, to demonstrate some teaching skill in order to try to build up the youngster's self-confidence and show him that despite the magnitude of the problems which our world faces, we still have the human and technological potential to bring about meaningful solutions. Parents can be guides, if only from a non-authoritarian distance. Furthermore, they can provide a shelter, a center of trust to which the youngster can turn in difficult moments.

They must not expect, however, to dominate the adolescent's life and views, or to be the focal point of his existence, for the adolescent must necessarily grow away from the family if he is to mature into an independent adult. A statistic taken from our study of young people in the New York area illuminates how increasingly in adolescence those outside the family gain ascendancy in their influence. Only four percent of our entire sample felt that their parents were the most important people in their lives. Thus, it would seem that the family forms a kind of human backdrop to the adolescent's development. If the family, per se, demands the central point on the stage, so many tensions are created that a great part of the youngster's energy is invested in rebellion; or it may mean that parents are overconcerned to a degree which stultifies maturation. A dialogue of trust between the generations can be developed only when parents learn to respect the adolescent's blossoming individuality and the concomitant need to move away from all the home may represent; and when adolescents begin to understand that their parents' attitudes toward them are based on genuine concern, and that the parental mode of life can be understood, and even justified, within an historical, social, and emotional context.

INDEX

H
See Heroin
Hallucinogens
See Hashish, LSD, Marijuana, Mescaline, Psilo-
cybin
Hanging loose, 72
Hash
See Hashish
Hashish, definition of, 115
See also Marijuana
Heroin, 49, 110-111, 129-131
description of high, 130
hazards of use, 130-131
history of use, 129-130
physical effects, 130
Hippies, 131-136
definition of, 114-115
Horse
See Heroin

Jargon, 94, 95, 96, 132
Junk
See Heroin

Laudanum, 112
See also Opium
"Loser" *vs.* "Winner" ideology, 98-100
LSD, 110-111, 115, 122-129, 130
description of high, 127-128
hazards of usage, 128-129
history of, 126
physical effects, 126-127
Lysergic Acid Diethylamide
See LSD

Marijuana, 110-111, 115, 122-126
as medicine, 123
description of high, 24-27, 124-125
hazards of usage, 125-126
physical effects, 123
Maryjane
See Marijuana